the coffee guide...
MELBOURNE

contributors...	3
introduction...	4
melbourne map...	5
what's the score...	6
city centre...	8
feature article CAFE TRENDS...	30
inner melbourne...	33
coffee roaster profile COFFEE SUPREME...	54
introducing THE TEA GUIDE...	93
outer melbourne...	118
feature article THE GOLDEN BEAN...	128
the coffee guide AWARDS...	154
directory...	158

We understand that there are many factors that go into making a great coffee. Our reviews take this into account and make allowance for these factors. We have taken all reasonable care in preparing this guide, we make no warranty about the accuracy or completeness of its content and, to the maximum extent permitted, disclaim all liability arising from its use.

First Published in 2010
Copyright © The Coffee Guide... Melbourne 2011
Printed In China

All rights reserved. No part of this book may be reproduced or transmitted in any form or by means, electronic or mechanical, including photocopying, recording or by any information storage and retrieval system, without prior permission in writing from the publisher. *The Australian Copyright Act 1968* (The Act) allows a maximum of one chapter or 10 per cent of this book, whichever is greater, to be photocopied by any educational institution (or body that administers it) has given a remuneration notice to Copyright Agency Limited (CAL) under the Act.

A Cataloguing-in-Publication entry is available from, The National Library of Australia
ISBN 978-0-9775664-6-4

the coffeeguide...
the guide to find...the perfect grind

PUBLISHER...
Guide Enterprises

EDITOR...
Hamish McDougall

WRITERS...

Selina Altomonte	Louise McCuskey
Rachel Berry	Hamish McDougall
Angela Cox	Kate Machin
Julie Dillon	Chris Moore
Gabriel Espinoza	Dan Neubronner
Jane de Graaff	Mark Scandurra
Julia Hebaiter	Mark Scruby
Jerrie Kaduthodil	Melinda Woledge

ARTISTIC TEAM...
Stacy Masiruw

Claudia Dinallo

The Tea Guide Designed By Squad Ink

Cover Photograph By Michael Marchment

The Coffee Guide...
PO Box 710
Five Dock NSW 2046
Australia

Fax: +61 2 9712 5594
Email: info@thecoffeeguide.com.au
Web: www.thecoffeeguide.com.au

INTRODUCTION

Well, it's been two years since our last edition — and how the cafe scene has changed in that short time (which of course felt like a Guide-less eternity). The coffee tragic of 2009 could be forgiven for feeling somewhat lost amid the sudden influx of Clovers, siphons, single estates and industrial chic... But never fear: our guide to the emergent trends of 2011 (page 30) will keep you in cafe vogue.

The two big additions to this relaunch edition (and you've doubtless spied them already, unless you're of that rare breed of readers who turn straight to the Introduction) are the 'Tea Guide' (page 93) and our inaugural Coffee Guide Awards. Never fear — we aren't surreptitious agents for a global tea conspiracy; but we have enjoyed the odd Assam in recent times, and wanted to share.

And the coffee stakes have risen with our coveted new awards (page 154), celebrating the caffeine highs of 2010-11.

Lastly, if like us you feel the sting of TCG's sporadic annual editions, visit us at thecoffeeguide.com.au — the best place to get wired online.

It's good to be back, and to be back for good.

Enjoy,

Team Coffee Guide...

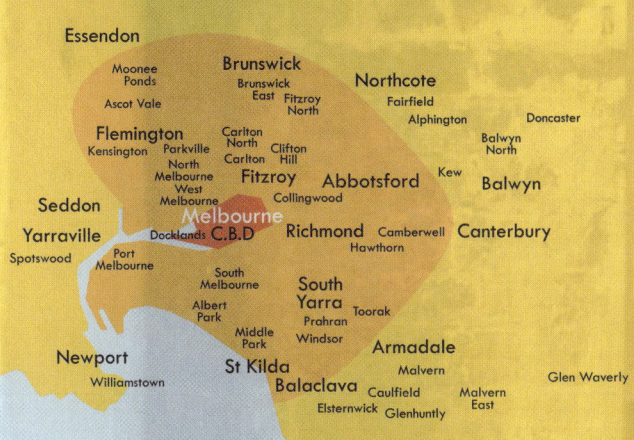

What's the score

Each of the cafes reviewed were awarded our unique 'Bean Rating'. The better the cafe, the more coffee beans it receives. Cafes were judged on two main components: the overall venue and the quality of their coffee. Each component consists of five categories, scored with a mark out of five, so each cafe received a total mark out of 50.

For each venue, two reviewers were sent out on different occasions to make their assessments. On each occasion at least two coffees were sampled, one being an espresso, the other a milk-based beverage. The average scores from both independent reviewers form the basis of the cafe's overall Bean Rating.

The different characteristics that were considered when rating the cafe are listed below and may seem overly technical at first, but are actually quite important when trying to distinguish the difference between a good coffee experience and a great coffee experience.

The following factors were rated out of five and totalled to gain a mark out of 25 for the quality of the venue:

- **Presentation:** what does the venue look like; does its appearance make it appealing?
- **Ambience:** how does a visit to the venue make you feel?
- **Service:** does the staff add or detract from the experience?
- **Cleanliness:** nobody likes dirty cups—prompt collection of plates and cups, general clutter and messiness are considered.
- **Menu:** what is on offer? The context of the cafe is considered in this assessment; for example, espresso bars or restaurants have a different take on what a menu should be. Does the menu suit the venue?

Similarly, the following factors were rated out of five and totalled to gain a mark out of 25 for the quality of the coffee:

- **Aroma:** refers to the strength and subtle variation between coffee smells. It can range from flowery and fruity, to nutty and spicy.
- **Acidity:** refers to the desirable dry sensation felt under the edges of your tongue. Its role in coffee is similar to its role in wine; it creates a sharp and vibrant element, which becomes flat when it is not present.
- **Body/Mouthfeel:** refers to the feeling of the coffee across your palate.

Your tongue can sense the coffee's heaviness, thickness and richness. It can be compared to the difference between a mouthful of water or full-cream milk. A good cup usually has a thick, creamy feel rather than being watery.

- **Flavour:** refers to the interplay between the acidity, aroma and body of the coffee. A rich flavour refers to the body and its fullness, while a complex flavour means there are multiple flavours being experienced. A balanced taste has no one sensation overpowering the others. Typical flavours may include fruity, nutty, spicy, sweet and earthy.

- **Aftertaste:** refers to the length of the sensation experienced after you swallow the coffee. It can range from being bitter to sweet and pleasant. It can either be short and sharp, or can be long and linger in your mouth.

These five features are what we use to determine a great cup of coffee. The ability to sense as well as describe the differences in taste and smell between different blends of coffee can dramatically improve the appreciation you have for your coffee, and will make you the envy of your friends. Imagine being able to tell the difference between Ethiopian and Indonesian coffee beans, know what an over-extracted coffee tastes like, or knowledgeably use such words as herby, caramelly and nutty to describe your sensations.

Bean rating

5 beans means a score of 46 or higher:
outstanding coffee, a definate place to go

4.5 beans means a score between 41 and 45

4 beans means a score between 36 and 40:
terrific coffee and worth a visit

3.5 beans means a score between 31 and 35

3 beans means a score between 26 and 30:
a respectable coffee is on offer in a pleasant setting

2.5 beans means a score between 21 and 25.

2 beans means a score between 16 and 20:
run of the mill and ordinary

DANCING GOAT
Shop 4/280 King Street, Melbourne

Before I'm even inside, I'm feeling somewhat redundant. You see, the front door of this hidden city cafe is plastered with reviews and press mentions. Fortunately, there's room (on the door) for one more.

A patient queue of corporates is another good sign, as is the shelf littered with awards and medals. They belong to Jess Hyde, a barista champion and part owner, and there's a star-struck excitement in waiting for my prize-winning espresso.

While the champ calls out orders and dances behind a chrome La Marzocco, I inspect an elaborate coffee tasting wheel, along with syphons and tampers for sale on a back wall. With the wheel's whirl of terms in my head, I take a sip of the espresso — perfect temperature, fragrant spice and chocolate aroma, well rounded mouthfeel and finish. It's a serious coffee, and you can see why so many reviewers are angling to write this place up. Hopefully Jess isn't yet tired of the same old rave reviews.

Phone
+ 613 9670 4002

Trading Hours
mon - fri: 7am - 4pm
saturday & sunday closed

Cafe... 19/25
Coffee... 20/25
Seven Seeds Specialty Coffee

QUIST'S COFFEE
166 Little Collins Street, Melbourne

Established in 1938, Quist's boasts that it's Melbourne's oldest coffee roasting house. Behind the window display of artfully arranged coffee equipment is a small shop, filled with an intoxicating coffee aroma — along with everything an aficionado could ask for. Friendly, knowledgeable staff guide buyers through the machines, plungers, percolators, cups and utensils, as well as the variety of roasted beans for sale.

This is a take-away venue only, and there's a steady stream of customers arriving for their caffeine hit (and complimentary almond biscuit). The floral and dark-chocolate notes of the Miscela Italiana blend shine through in an elegant espresso. There is a lightness that should not be mistaken for wateriness. My latte, smelling of toasted nuts, is equally good: the rich, creamy flavour bursts onto the tongue, with a pleasant aftertaste. These are coffees to savour — so find a nearby seat and enjoy.

Phone
+613 9650 1530

Trading Hours
mon - fri: 9am - 5pm
saturday & sunday closed

Cafe... 22/25
Coffee... 22/25
Quist's Coffee

65 DEGREES
309 Exhibition Street, Melbourne

The north-eastern end of Exhibition Street seems an unlikely home for a world champion barista. But even though it's away from the main CBD shopping strips, this small cafe is a hit with those in the know. Simply follow the smell of roasted beans to find some of the best coffee in Melbourne.

The narrow but light-filled interior offers a few tables, where a decent breakfast and lunch menu is chalked on a blackboard. Decent, yes, but it's always going to play second fiddle to the coffee — and Con Haralambopoulos's skills. One of three brothers behind the cafe, Con has won world espresso and latte art champion titles. And it shows.

Warm cocoa notes dominate in a smooth and silky short black. The latte is simply stunning: there's a hint of roasted almonds but no flavour predominates in the smooth, balanced brew that slips down without effort. This is a must-visit destination.

Phone
+613 9662 1080

Trading Hours
mon - fri: 6am - 4pm
saturday & sunday closed

Cafe... 22/25
Coffee... 24/25
Gridlock Coffee

PELLEGRINI'S
66 Bourke Street, Melbourne

A veritable Melbourne icon, Pellegrini's has been serving up generous portions of home-style Italy for decades. The owner proudly proclaims that Pellegrini's had "the first real espresso machine in Melbourne", which isn't hard to believe when you spy the décor — with its old-school wood veneer and utilitarian furnishings. Today, a Vittoria-branded Faema E91 Diplomat looms on the bench.

The espresso comes in a traditional demitasse, with a solid crema. A spicy aroma arises — typical of Vittoria coffee. Also typical is the almost complete lack of nuance, traded instead for raw caffeine horsepower and brute force. If you crave a morning heart-starter and aren't looking for subtlety, this is the place for you. Even the latte is as subtle as a brick through a plate-glass window. This is, however, one of the few places that could be forgiven for its lack of nuance: Pellegrini's doesn't try to be anything more than a traditional Italian Espresso bar with Italian home-style dishes. Don't ask for fine dining — you'll just be met with confused looks and knockout coffee.

Phone
+613 9662 1885

Trading Hours
mon - sat: 8am - 11.30pm
sun: 12pm - 8pm

Cafe... 20/25
Coffee... 15/25
Vittoria

RED CUP CAFE
120 Collins Street, Melbourne

With no signage or street presence, this coffee bar in the light-filled foyer of a Collins Street skyscraper caters more to office workers than to passing traffic. The fit-out is slick corporate: tastefully muted cream, black and greys mingle with low-slung leather couches, perfect for meetings. Perhaps because of the cathedral-like dimensions, there's little background noise but still a sense of atmosphere.

Courteous staff, clad in stylish grey aprons, greet regulars by name, and the queues are long at peak times. However, the coffee is expensive ($3.80 for a regular) and uneven. My espresso is puckeringly bitter, its smoky aroma matched by a tarry taste. The latte, tasted on a separate visit, is creamy and less bitter but very hot. With cheaper and better coffee nearby, this place is better suited to caffeine-hit corporates than to dedicated coffee hunters.

Phone
+613 9663 9503

Trading Hours
mon - fri: 7am - 4.30pm
saturday & sunday closed

Cafe... 16/25
Coffee... 9/25
Di Bella Coffee

BAMBINI BARISTA
Shop T7/530 Little Collins Street, Melbourne

Bambini Barista is located in the heart of the CBD, in the Exchange Tower building that looks like a hotel lobby. Bambini is one of a few cafes crammed into this foyer — competing for your $3 and that illustrious slice of the coffee market.

The financial crisis might be global, but over at Bambini, the queues of office types suggest we're not ready to forgo our morning coffee just yet.

I somehow secure one of the tables – scarce, despite most patrons opting for takeaway – and my espresso arrives promptly. The shot has a soft, velvety mouthfeel and fills this small part of the enormous lobby with a mild toffee aroma. Subtle acidity supports the earthy, ashy flavour. Milk-based beverages are the norm at this cafe. The cappuccino that follows has a thick foam over a medium body. The toffee fragrance from the shot cuts through, while the acidity is tamed by the milk. The aftertaste is a mix of bittersweet notes.

Phone
+613 9614 0023

Trading Hours
mon - fri: 7.30am - 4.30pm
saturday & sunday closed

Cafe... 17/25
Coffee... 15/25
Grinders Coffee

TWO FINGERS
27 Russell Street, Melbourne

As befits a cafe in the shadows of the Moorish-style Forum Theatre, Two Fingers is theatrically styled. The cosy narrow shop has three Parisian-style round tables and a banquette at the front, and red leather couches at the back, half-hidden by the staircase leading up to a lounge area.

With red patterned wallpaper, lamps to light the darkly intimate interior and well-stocked liquor shelves, it feels more like a bar than a cafe. But the coffee machine and daily changing menu – tortillas and roti wraps, on our visit – bring it back to cafe country.

Espressos are served in vintage china cups, the tarry aroma giving way to dark chocolate notes with a long aftertaste. The latte is nutty but slightly thin and weak with no aftertaste; but it's not unpleasant. And this is a thoroughly enjoyable, and very Melbourne, venue.

Phone
+613 9663 0202

Trading Hours
mon - thur: 7am - 5pm
fri: 7am - 11pm
sat: 9am - 3pm
sunday closed

Cafe... 21/25
Coffee... 19/25
Genovese Coffee

COFFEE HQ
367 Collins Street, Melbourne

Melbourne commuters will be familiar with the Coffee HQ carts and outlets at train stations around the CBD and suburbs. Coffee HQ is the company's first cafe-style premises where one can pull up a chair and relax while enjoying the eponymous blend. It's located in the foyer of the Optus Building in Collins Street, where an overhead atrium provides uplifting sunlight that office workers would appreciate. There's also outdoor seating.

My espresso is a tad watery, but exhibits complex flavours ranging from caramel through to bitter chocolate, with a spicy aroma. It's bitey and bitter at first, before resolving into a mild burnt-toast aftertaste — especially at the back of the palate. The latte is competent, with tangy and tart flavours and a comforting toffee aroma.

Breakfast and lunch options are ready-to-go muffins, biscuits, croissants and sandwiches. I'd hesitate to call this cafe a destination in itself, but it's a good option if you're in town and you need quick and reliable caffeination.

Phone
+613 9621 2260

Trading Hours
mon - fri: 7am - 5pm
saturday & sunday closed

Cafe... 20/25
Coffee... 18/25
Veneziano

LUDO CAFE
118 Queen Street, Melbourne

The happy hum of the lunch crowd in this Monday-to-Friday CBD cafe speaks volumes about the quality of its coffee — not to mention its selection of panini and pastries. Feed them and caffeinate them and they will come.

Ludo offers reasonably-priced breakfast and lunch standards – porridge, panini, soups – and options such as soy and extra shots are available for the coffees. You can even sneak in a glass of wine before heading back to your 2.30pm conference call. The décor is simple and welcoming; there's some art on the walls and ambience is cheerful and unpretentious.

Allpress coffee jolts workers into action in the mornings and helps them stay awake through the afternoon's gnarled spreadsheets. My espresso has an immediate bite and is sour on the tongue. But it's also rich and frothy, and develops into a medium-to-long biscuit and tobacco aftertaste. The aroma is nutty and grainy, with burnt toast overtones. My latte is strong and well-made, with robust nutty and bready flavours, and an excellent crema.

Phone
+613 9670 9488

Trading Hours
mon - fri: 7am - 5pm
saturday & sunday closed

Cafe... 19/25
Coffee... 20/25
Allpress Espresso

Photographs kindly provided by Sensory Lab.

SENSORY LAB
David Jones, 297 Little Collins Street, Melbourne

Sensory Lab is not so much a cafe as a coffee experience. The brainchild of the folks behind St Ali, the Lab offers nine coffees (four blends and five single origins) and four brewing methods (including siphon, pour over and cold drip), encouraging customers to broaden their palates as well as their minds.

Sensing this is not the time to stick with my customary latte, I abandon myself to a lab coated barista, who prepares a siphoned Ethiopian Yirgacheffe. The result is a delicate, tea-like brew with a floral aroma and jasmine flavour. Light in acidity, there is virtually no mouthfeel and the finish is short and sweet. By contrast, My S3 blend espresso has a deeply complex flavour, underpinned by touches of honey and cocoa. Thick on the tongue, with a medium acidity, it delivers an intensely sweet finish.

While Sensory Lab is not a place to linger – both seating and food options are limited – caffeinistas will appreciate the wow factor, not to mention the gorgeous Slayer machine. Time to experiment.

Phone
+613 9686 2990

Trading Hours
mon - wed: 9.30am - 6pm
thur - fri: 9.30am - 9pm
sat: 9am - 7pm
sun: 10am - 6pm

Cafe... 21/25
Coffee... 20/25
Sensory Lab Coffee

STAX
16 Little LaTrobe Street, Melbourne

You'd expect this sort of Melbourne establishment in a random alley featuring a lone Korean restaurant, an art supplies shop and buildings doused with graffiti. It's where we're automatically drawn for our caffeine fixes.

There's not much in the way of interior décor — aside from the generous display of posters for local events and the barista's credentials, showcased on a blackboard. Oh, and this is apparently the poster cafe for Genovese coffee, with badged paraphernalia everywhere. The bubbly waitress happily writes us out the name of the music resonating from her iPod (Buddha Bar II: Dinner). And speaking of food, the menu du jour includes a delightful, slow-cooked lamb ragu.

That 'man does not live by coffee alone' rings true in this case. The fabulous service, culinary gusto and enticing nutty fragrance of the espresso are enough to override its acidic sharpness and prolonged astringent conclusion — symptomatic of an over-extraction.

Phone
+613 9663 3008

Trading Hours
mon - fri: 7.30am - 4pm
saturday & sunday closed

Cafe... 17/25
Coffee... 12/25
Genovese Coffee

THE MESS HALL
51 Bourke Street, Melbourne

The Mess Hall is a modern Italian cafe exuding raw funkiness. Many of the original fittings have been retained, while the furniture affords an almost Tuscan feel, with earthy colours and rustic woods. It's a great spot to relax and watch the world go by.

The menu is very Italian, but with a modern take. The light and crisp Whitebait Fries, just like the decor, offer an ingenuous mix of old and new.

The espresso is presented in a simple but chunky demitasse, and a rich brown crema licks up the sides. With a flowery aroma, the espresso has a very strong front palate, matched by its acidity. It falls away from there to almost no rear palate at all and a short finish. A sharp shot indeed — almost overpowering.

The latte comes with an expertly formed rosetta. Even through the milk, the acidity shines. Fortunately, the finish is rounded by the milk, providing a more mellow experience.

Phone
+613 9654 6800

Trading Hours
mon - fri: 7am - 5pm
sat - sun: 8am - 10pm

Cafe... 20/25
Coffee... 14/25
Romcaffe

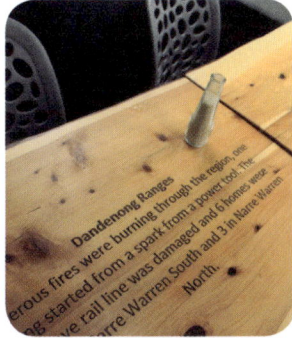

City Centre

ESPRESSINO
Rialto Building, 68 King Street, Melbourne

This sophisticated Italian cafe and pizzeria is situated in the Rialto building, and certainly befits the business end of town. Patrons can watch corporate life go by from the vantage point of a large open courtyard on the corner of King and Collins Streets, or escape into the modern, minimalist but cheery room inside.

A visual and gastronomic focal point is the wide range of pizzette (available for breakfast and lunch) in a large glass cabinet. They come served on wooden boards, and the Eggplant and Cherry Tomato Pizzetta is pure joy. And there's an equally tantalising array of panini, piadine, salads and dolci.

On the coffee side of the equation, my espresso looks picture-perfect in a bright orange cup, with a honey-coloured crema. It's somewhat watery, but packs a punch, bursting with spices, roasted nuts and caramel notes with a long and lovely aftertaste. My latte has the same good looks and taste complexity. The perfect business pit-stop.

Phone
+613 9620 4774

Trading Hours
mon - fri: 7am - 5pm
saturday & sunday closed

Cafe... 19/25
Coffee... 18/25
Padre Coffee

COFFEA COFFEE
521 Elizabeth Street, Melbourne

This place is all about shopping bags, jeeps, prams, and generations coming together around the huge bean-blending apparatus that dominates the room. For a decade, Coffea has been serving up coffee and sustenance to foot-sore Victoria Market shoppers, as well as roasting and blending take-home beans — Fair Trade Organic and Nicaraguan, to name just two. Cabinets of goodies promise zucchini fritters, thick sandwiches, rhubarb and polenta cake, and much more.

We order an espresso and affogato from the bustling counter. The former is well-rounded and smooth to taste, resolving on the palate to produce more than a hint of nutty, burnt crust. The aroma is slightly tangy and reminiscent of raisin toast, however, its middle-of-the-road viscosity tends toward the watery. By contrast, the affogato is a creamy, coffee and ice-cream treat that strikes a good balance between the espresso and the cold stuff, and has an enticing rum-and-raisin aroma.

Coffea is a great place to nurse your purchases before hopping on a tram and heading home.

Phone
+613 9326 7388

Trading Hours
tue - sat: 7am - 3pm
sun: 9am - 3pm
monday closed

Cafe... 19/25
Coffee... 19/25
Coffea Coffee

D'MARCO'S ESPRESSO BAR
The Paramount Centre, 108 Bourke Street, Melbourne

Great coffee in Chinatown is as rare as dim sum in Little Italy. Bucking the trend, however, is D'Marco's. Established in 2003 by brothers Dominic and Marco, this exceptional cafe is a forerunner of the city's espresso bar trend.

After ordering, I squeeze past a queue of office workers (many are greeted by name) to snare one of only three tables inside the tiny space. I am soon transported to a homely place in '60s Rome. It's all dim lighting, smooth jazz, burgundy velvet, dark wood, vintage Mario Lanza posters, well-used kitchen items (such as a coffee mill), aged books and black and white photos of family members (including the owners' father, an old hand at Pellegrini's).

My espresso, promptly delivered, continues the journey. Its thick golden crema is matched by a wonderfully spicy aroma. A bright acidity is balanced by dark chocolate notes that linger on the palate. With milk, the blend is even more luscious and the sweet aftertaste eases my return to the toils of the day.

Phone
+613 9639 3976

Trading Hours
mon - fri: 7am - 5pm
saturday & sunday closed

Cafe... 18/25
Coffee... 19/25
Vittoria

ROAST AND BREW
530 Collins Street, Melbourne

Majestic columns, marble walls and huge windows lend an air of grandeur to this cafe — lodged in the light-filled base of a busy financial and legal commercial tower. Despite the soaring ceilings and vast open space, the area has a buzz, with plenty of foot traffic, and King Street outside provides a suitably frenetic backdrop.

Office workers use the array of smart tables, chairs and couches for caffeine-fuelled meetings, and there's a takeaway queue. The friendly staff and baristas know most of the customers by name and are quick to whip up "the usual".

Despite the guaranteed client base from the building, the coffee here stands on its own merits. My espresso sings with buttery and toasty notes, its slightly bitter aftertaste lingering pleasantly, while a rich and creamy latte is full of caramelised nuts. Definitely worth a visit if you're at this end of town — and especially if you occupy a rival tower.

Phone
+613 9620 9390

Trading Hours
mon - fri: 6.30am - 4.30pm
saturday & sunday closed

Cafe... 19/25
Coffee... 20/25
Green Bean Espresso

ECLIPSE
Shop 7a/495 Collins Street, Melbourne

Don't be fooled by the address: the entrance is in fact on Flinders Lane, hidden away at the back of the refurbished Intercontinental Hotel. Red-brick walls surround a nightclub-like interior, its darkness illuminated by spotlights on the walls. The serving area and Synesso machine dominate the small interior, and return us to the coffee scene.

Queues are long in peak hours, but the city-chic staff are quick and gracious under pressure. Although most customers are there for takeaway, there's ample reason to eat in, with a few small tables, pastries and a lovely lunch menu.

And then there's the excellent coffee. My aromatic espresso is powerful and rich, with unsweetened cocoa and luxurious woody notes. The toastier, nuttier latte is equally masterful, a balanced blend of chocolaty coffee with creamy milk that slips down very easily. A relative newcomer to the CBD coffee scene, Eclipse has already overshadowed nearby rivals, and promises to be a stayer.

Phone
+613 9629 7703

Trading Hours
mon - fri: 6.30am - 6pm
saturday & sunday closed

Cafe... 20/25
Coffee... 20/25
Eclipse Blend

Cumulus Inc.
McNabb Gomes Architects
Photography John Gollings

CUMULUS INC.
45 Flinders Lane, Melbourne

Despite its high-end reputation, Cumulus Inc. is warm, welcoming, and entirely without any pretension. Its buzzy vibe and excellent staff complement a funky layout, and light streams in through original steel-framed windows.

There's a leather banquette along one wall and wooden tables in the centre, while solo diners or couples can choose from a round communal table or the marble bar overlooking the busy, quietly efficient kitchen.

Chef Andrew McConnell is justifiably famous for his superb food, but as much care and attention is paid to the coffee here. Made with Single Origin beans from Sydney, the espresso has an enticing fruity aroma. It has an intense flavour with notes of unsweetened cocoa and a touch of berries. The latte is lighter and more mellow, with caramel and nuts blended into the creamy milk. Got to love a restaurant that respects the bean — come for the food but linger for the coffee.

Phone
+613 9650 1445

Trading Hours
mon - fri: 7am - 11pm
sat - sun: 8am - 11pm

Cafe... 23/25
Coffee... 22/25
Single Origin Roasters

City Centre

JUNGLE JUICE BAR
20 Centre Place, Melbourne

It's a jungle out there — the wilds of Melbourne lanes crammed full of cafes and peak-hour patrons struggling for a seat. But this shoebox cafe is well worth the expedition.

Lurking under the grungy bar Hell's Kitchen, Jungle Juice has a similar vibe and cool young crowd who are happy to sit more or less on each other's laps — once they're lucky and funky enough to get in. Today I'm neither, so I order my espresso to go from the laneway window which supports a La Marzocco Linea.

My espresso hit of St Ali is exactly what the medicine man ordered, with bright acid, a fruity aroma and lingering chocolaty finish. I slam it down with barely enough time to put money on the counter, before I'm swept down the lane by the hungry hordes, like a floating log in the Amazon River. Next time I'll pitch camp inside.

Phone
+613 9639 8779

Trading Hours
everyday: 7am - 5pm

Cafe... 16/25
Coffee... 18/25
St Ali Specialty Roasters

NEGRONI
477 Collins Street, Melbourne

Walking into Negroni feels like I've just crashed a stranger's wedding. I can't recall seeing so many well-pressed Italian suits in one place, except for maybe a Peter Jackson advertisement. Feeling under-dressed for the occasion, I can't help but check myself out in a floor-to-ceiling collage of gold-framed antique mirrors. The interior designer must have been Liberace. Opulence brewed with extravagance is the only way to describe this place, and the décor is slick European, with black marble, mahogany timber and leather, and black chandeliers in each room taking centre stage.

The coffee — Giancarlo blend by Grinders. My espresso arrives with a pale golden crema and nutty, toffee aroma. Mild citrus notes precede a pleasant bitter-chocolate finish.

And as the evening approaches and the lights dim, I find myself sinking into a worn leather couch, then ordering a namesake cocktail to de-stress from all this excitement.

Phone
+613 9614 1319

Trading Hours
mon - fri: 7am - 10pm
saturday & sunday closed

Cafe... 18/25
Coffee... 16/25
Giancarlo By Grinders

COFFEE HQ FLINDERS STREET STATION
Kiosk 1/207 Flinders Street, Melbourne

Right in the middle of Flinders Street Station, Coffee HQ advertises itself as a tiny coffee island in a sea of pedestrian traffic. This squat, heavily-branded box shop is difficult to miss, as are the two bright red La Marzocco espresso machines which lie within.

The staff are all smiles — and acclimatised to talking at a higher volume to cope with the noise of the train station. There are a collection of picnic tables nearby that everyone shares. This makes a great spot to enjoy my Coffee HQ espresso and BLT sandwich.

My espresso features a caramel aroma with a hint of spice, followed by high levels of acidity with a slight sweetness at the end. Balanced, yet with a low viscosity, and short, clean finish. The latte tones down the acidity of the shot. The sweetness in the espresso is accentuated by the milk. Sugar-junkies might consider halving their spoonfuls in order to appreciate this natural sweetness.

Phone
+613 9621 2260

Trading Hours
mon - sat: 6am - 11pm
sun: 6am - 9pm

Cafe... 17/25
Coffee... 18/25
Veneziano

PUSHKA ESPRESSO BAR
20 Pesgrave Avenue, Melbourne

Melbourne is renowned for its hidden treasures down graffitoed laneways, and Pushka makes this concept fresh and fun. This hole-in-the-wall cafe is barely spacious enough for four tables and a narrow bar, but that's part of the charm. Situated in an alley off a laneway, it's also a miniature art gallery.

A small breakfast and lunch menu showcases food that's easy to prepare in a miniscule kitchen (think bagels, piadinas and baguettes), plus there's a small wine and beer list.

The staff are friendly and knowledgeable. The barista recommends a Sumatran single origin blend for a latte. It's a good choice: the complex mix of flavours is initially buttery and caramelly, but there's an underlying dark-chocolate note. This coffee rewards slow sipping. My espresso, made with the house blend from Syndicate, is bright and smooth, with a long, sweet aftertaste.

Trading Hours
mon - wed: 8am - 7pm
thur - fri: 8am - 11pm
saturday & sunday closed

Cafe... 20/25
Coffee... 20/25
Syndicate Espresso

CAFENATICS
387 Flinders Lane, Melbourne

For many aficionados, chain-store coffee equals bad coffee. But Cafenatics, which has six outlets around the CBD, bucks the trend. This store, in the art nouveau-style Tavistock House building, is light and bright inside, with more seats in the brick-walled courtyard.

The food is excellent: pre-made focaccia and wraps are supplemented by specials from the commercial kitchen — think pasta or meatballs — along with muffins, brownies and Italian doughnuts to satisfy sweeter cravings. This is the only Cafenatics with a liquor licence — but let's not get distracted from the coffee.

A chocolate scent wafts from my short black, and there's a strong taste of berries that lingers, long and sweet. My latte smells nutty, but no one flavour dominates in the thick, creamy brew. The palate sings with the harmony of a balanced coffee that slips down like silk.

Phone
+613 9614 0995

Trading Hours
mon - fri: 6.30am - 5pm
saturday & sunday closed

Cafe... 20/25
Coffee... 20/25
Veneziano

SOCIAL ROASTING COMPANY
5 Makillop Street, Melbourne

This place couldn't be more socially or environmentally responsible if it tried. Not only is the coffee 100 per cent ethically sourced, but the cafe is also part of Fair Business, a non-profit organisation providing jobs for the long-term unemployed. The team even delivers fresh beans to offices via pedal power, thanks to their big green bikes. How cool is that?

But it's not only the feel-good factor that makes SRC a winner. The atmosphere is pleasantly casual, with a retro-ethnic feel, and a blackboarded wall lists some tasty and innovative breakfasts. Once you've ordered, the vintage Probat roaster in the corner adds a touch of interest.

The piny aroma of the espresso pre-empts its own arrival at the table. This is knock-your-socks-off stuff: the thick, dark crema gives way to a tangy, viscous brew with a pleasant but mouth-puckering acidity and a long, long finish. The latte is similarly robust, the milk adding a velvety smoothness without diminishing the flavour. This is coffee at its finest.

Phone
+613 9600 2577

Trading Hours
mon - fri: 7am - 4pm
sat - sun: 8am - 4pm

Cafe... 18/25
Coffee... 20/25
Social Roasting Company

HOME BARISTA INSTITUTE
51 Queen Street, Melbourne

Dodging office-workers in the city streets, I make my way to the foyer of a modern Queen Street building where the Home Barista Institute resides. Passers-by are lured in by a huge plasma screen showing coffee after coffee being poured by a steady hand, like a caffeinated piper to the city's corporate children.

Inside, it's a modern affair with plenty of wood panelling and timber tables. Flyers and brochures are strewn across the tables, advertising courses on coffee-making that take just four hours — and presumably last you a coffee-drinking lifetime.

But I don't have time for that; I need my espresso now. A hit of mild acidity with toffee and walnut characteristics come with the espresso. With a light body and muted, short-lived finish, I need another hit. So I try a flat white. Ah yes, that's good. Well textured milk and perfect temperature. Those toffee and nut characteristics cut through the milk and leave a pleasant finish on the palate. With a name like Home Barista Institute, you expect to leave with a bachelor of coffee. For my few dollars, all I get is a takeaway flatty — although it's a graduation of sorts.

Phone
+613 9629 7350

Trading Hours
mon - fri: 7am - 3pm
saturday & sunday closed

Cafe... 19/25
Coffee... 17/25

Home Barista Institute Blend

BROTHER BABA BUDAN
359 Little Bourke Street, Melbourne

Passion broods within this coffee den. There's a progressive yet weathered, street-beat grunge mellowing beneath the chairs that cluster on the ceiling. White-collar workers grab takeaway and take off through the silver scoop-handled door, while others sit around long into the day.

Where the décor pays wall-papered homage to coffee's ancient origins, the baristas themselves are a modern production line of efficiency as they work through an unabating order list. A small selection of sweet, crumbling morsels is enticing, but doesn't distract from the star performer — the coffee, available in espresso or Clover filter form.

Inhaling the house espresso is akin to sitting upwind of a thick clove grove; on the palate, it washes around with a ricocheting acidity. My latte melts like a butterscotch pastille, and its jasmine insinuations unlock a world of coffee pleasure — much as Baba Budan broke the Turks' coffee-tree monopoly when he smuggled out those seven precious seeds.

Phone
+613 9606 0449

Trading Hours
mon - sat: 7am - 5pm
sunday closed

Cafe... 22/25
Coffee... 22/25
Seven Seeds Specialty Coffee

SWITCHBOARD
Manchester Unity Arcade, 220 Collins Street, Melbourne

The Manchester Unity Building in Melbourne fairly drips with 1930s Neo-Gothic charm. The Switchboard is tucked away in a minor walkway (with glorious original floor tiles) that connects the glorious heritage-listed foyer with some fancy frock shops. The cafe dispenses great coffee, satisfying soup and toasted sarnies to those who've sought out, or stumbled upon, this beguiling establishment.

Coffee Supreme beans are used here, and the espresso action happens in an alcove above a delightful display of cupcakes (on a cake-stand, ladies). My espresso boasts significant, but not objectionable, acidity and hints at slightly burnt toast before rounding out to a more robust rye-bread finish — helped along by middle-of-the-road viscosity. It eventually resolves to a sweet finish and all the flavours linger long on the palate. My latte is served at just the right temperature with a creamy demeanour and hints of sugary nuttiness — no need for extra sweetener.

Trading Hours
mon - fri: 7am - 4pm
saturday & sunday closed

Cafe... 21/25
Coffee... 21/25
Coffee Supreme

Want to be a five bean café?

In an increasingly competitive market place make sure you're equipment isn't letting you down. The Synesso family of espresso machines combine market leading temperature stability and clever design with the barista in mind. Well designed and well supported, this is one staff member you can rely upon.

Find out why the leading cafes around the world use Synesso.

Contact: Ben Bicknell
Email: ben.bicknell@fivesenses.com.au
Mobile: 0439 511 881
Five Senses Roastery: (03) 5975 5221

Five Senses Coffee
- Exclusive distributor of Synesso in Australia

www.fivesenses.com.au

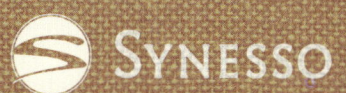

5 SENSES
COFFEE

BROOD BOX
8 Rankins Lane, Melbourne

Brood Box Gallery epitomises three things that Melbourne does extremely well: it celebrates emerging artists; brings a 19th-Century laneway to life; and rustles up a great coffee.

The gallery itself is a cool, high-ceilinged space that opens out to the laneway via a roller door. A focal point – apart from the art, of course – is the old spray-painted caravan that has been kitted out with coffee-making paraphernalia and a cheerful barista.

The espresso is presented on a stainless steel tray and comes with a small glass of sparkling mineral water. Nice touch. The coffee's sweet, complex flavour evolves well, starting off sharp and spicy before becoming mellow and slightly dulled (a bit like a good night out). The caramel and biscuit notes come through between sips of palate-cleansing mineral water. The latte chaser is just right: St Ali beans turn into a sweet, creamy treat crafted by a skilled man in a caravan.

Phone
+613 9670 8822

Trading Hours
mon - fri: 7am - 5pm
sat: 10am - 4pm
sunday closed

Cafe... 22/25
Coffee... 22/25
St Ali Specialty Roasters

LIAISON
22 Ridgway Place, Melbourne

Monaco House by architects McBride Charles Ryan is a fabulous and prismatic jumble of design derring-do. It's way cool, and so is Liaison — the shiny smiley cafe housed in the bottom of it. Liaison is yet another cafe up a city laneway, but this one is like stepping into the glossy and groovy pages of Wallpaper* or Monocle.

Not only does it look great, but Liaison's chirpy staff also make great coffee. My latte is rich and strong, with a toffee and biscuit aroma. It's slightly and nicely bitter, and topped with a rich crema. My espresso is similarly rewarding, with a tobacco aroma and lots of fruity, well-rounded flavours. It's clean-tasting, with rich viscosity and hardly any grit.

As the name suggests, this is the place for a cosy breakfast or lunch of pastries and sandwiches — before heading back to the office with an illicit skip in your step.

Trading Hours
mon - fri: 7am - 4pm
saturday & sunday closed

Cafe... 19/25
Coffee... 18/25
Genovese Coffee

City Centre

THE CUP OF TRUTH (C.O.T)
12 Campbell Arcade, Degraves Street, Melbourne

This cafe-bar – a tiny hole in the wall down in the subway linking Flinders Street station to Degraves Street – is a godsend for the caffeine-needy underground commuter.

The morning queue is handy, as awakening brains may take a while to decide between the Ethiopian Yirgacheffe and the daily house blend. Nonetheless, the efficient owner-barista duo Courtney and Verity (ex Vue de Monde) elicit a decision and set the Synesso to work on my African beans.

The fruity aroma of my espresso is an immediate boost, but it's the wild acidity and dazzling lemon and lime notes that cures the Mondayitis. The latte is equally uplifting; the soft texture and sweet creaminess of the milk complement the wildness of the Brazilian house blend, and a heavenly dark chocolate bitterness lingers on the palate. Without a doubt, it's worth descending into Melbourne's infernal commuter depths for this superlative devil's cup.

Trading Hours
mon - thur: 7am - 5pm
fri: 7am - 4pm
saturday & sunday closed

Cafe... 20/25
Coffee... 20/25
5 Senses Coffee

You visited the Cafe...
You tried the coffee...
Don't you think it's time to make it at home?

GRAB the best BEANS by the best ROASTERS

www.thecoffee

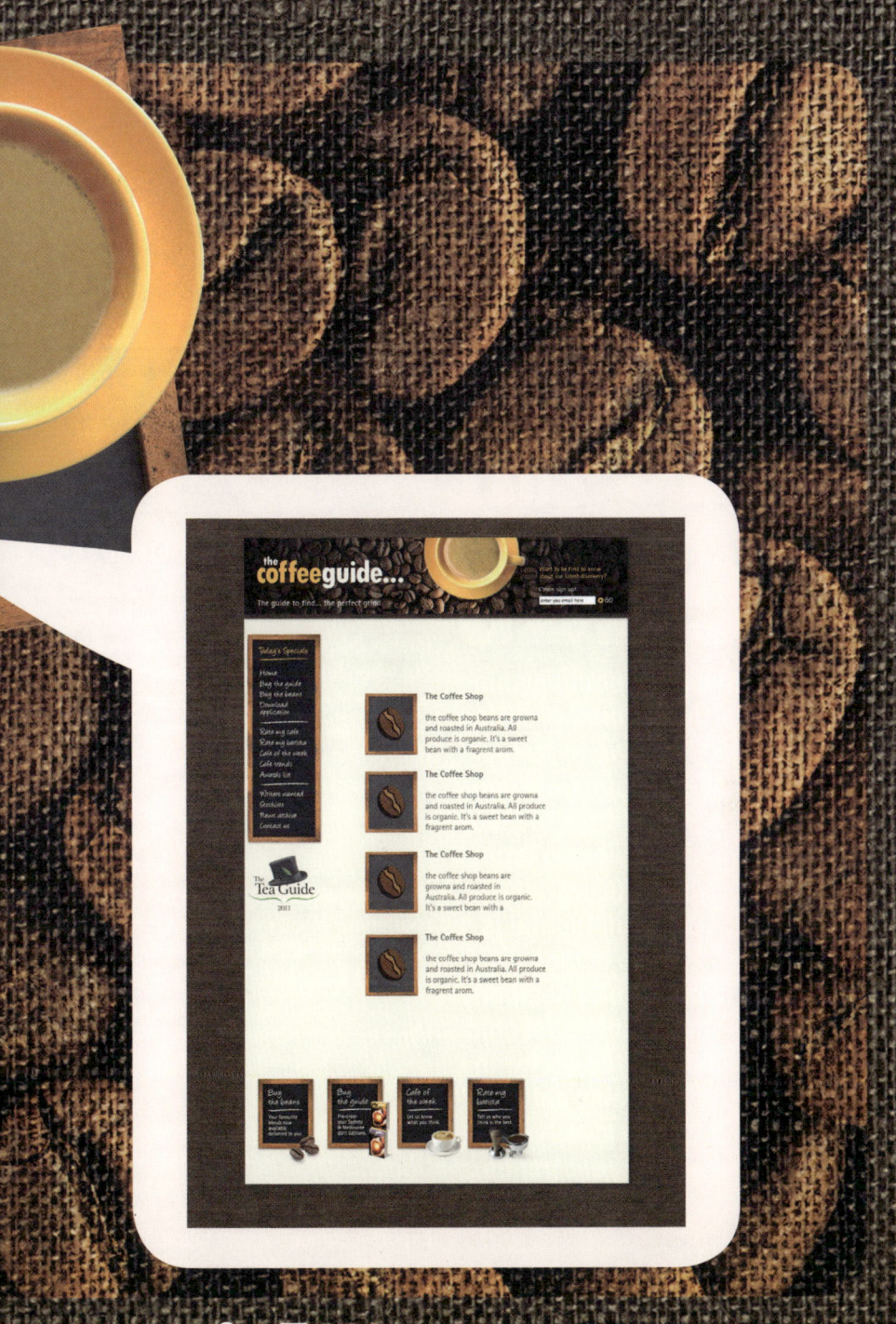

guide.com.au

Café 2011 Trends

Like just about anything worth consuming, coffee is slave to fashion. We've gone from caps and lattes to macs and piccolo lattes, while musing how the urban industrial is a more human (read comfortable) aesthetic than minimalist chic. So what's next for the caffeine catwalk? TCG gives you the emergent trends...

Rise of the customised blend

Imported coffee blends are out, as locals continue to outperform them thanks to fresher beans brewed at their optimal time. But when luxury becomes commonplace, and 'freshly roasted' is no longer the rarity but the rule, cafes have to turn to signature blends to maintain their place in the pressurised coffee scene.

The House Blend has made its home in Sydney/Melbourne cafes, as boutique roasters cook up signature styles that stand out from the growing tide of run-of-the-mill roasteries. When everybody's touting sassy banter and industrial chic, it's time to pluck out the 11 secret herbs and spices.

Expect more and more cafes to put their hand up for a signature blend — TCG, for one, thinks they're finger-licking good.

Exhibitionism

As the coffee takes centre stage (while food and reunions bugger off to the suburbs), the limelight is shining brightly on the barista. Expect theatrics – presentation, ceramics, latte art – and moreover, machines out front. They're noisy, steamy, distracting — like late night television. And instead of being hidden behind bars or at the

photograph supplied by Market Lane Coffee

back of the room, they'll be on display, and the barista likewise.

And why not? Coffee itself has moved from greaser of conversational wheels to outright showpiece, and now roasters, machines and grinders are following suit. Time we all discovered baristas have names — and, moreover, moves.

Stand and deliver

Okay, so we're going out on a limb on this one... We've ditched the Italian-style coffee, but we're about to usher in the Italian espresso bar — stocked with fresh Aussie roasts, of course.

Thanks to the customised blend, there'll be fewer of those branded umbrellas, seats and windbreakers around, and courtesy of that exhibitionistic streak, we all want a piece of the action.

Italians don't fumble through the cold wobbling hot coffee to their chapped lips. They drink inside, standing up. And with that many sassy Australian baristas around, we're surprised this hasn't already exploded. As coffee drinkers increasingly appreciate the likes of customised blends and single origins, they'll want to sip them in peace – or at least while chatting at an espresso bar – rather than dosing up on caffeine like a dietary supplement on the city streets.

Just as buying a morning coffee is already a routine for most of us, drinking it will become one two. In the next year or so, expect standing masses taking espressos (etc) at the bar for $3 a cup.

Single origin

For years, Australian roasters have been chasing the perfect blend — meticulously adjusting beans and percentages to deliver the idyllic combination of cream, body, acid and flavour. Now, as the explosion of boutique roasters pushes us ever closer to truly divine blends, we've dumped them for single origins.

Well, not exactly. But they are stealing the show, as more and more cafés offer a single origin coffee, or even a 'single of the day', to entice caffeine trendites into new and exciting brews. Where once we coveted balance, the single origin promotes signature flavours: the strong accent of geography coming through in Ethiopian earthiness, the heavy oils of a Sumatran, or citric Costa Ricans.

They don't cater to everyone, but single origins are an interesting and endlessly chic alternative to middle-of-the-road blends — with our apologies to the roasters.

Black is the new black

Latte fever has run its course, and the rise of local roasters and boutique blends is swelling the ranks of espresso purists. But in an interesting twist, we're also seeing a greater variety of brewing methods, in particular, the Clover and siphon.

Clover

This is a fairly recent addition to the coffee-machine arsenal, designed in the American home of coffee, Seattle, in the hope of glamourising the long black. The fiddliness of the machine — baristas can specify the temperature (to a tenth of a degree) and brewing time — contrasts the simplicity of the output: a delicate long black, without milk, froth, or Seattle-style flavouring.

Similarly, the Clover may look like a simple black box, but inside is a series of pipes and chambers, in which vacuums and pistons steep, agitate and filter the coffee with gentle meticulousness. Where espresso can stress beans and strip flavours, Clover is subtlety itself — which is why Anthony Svilicich, of Sydney's Le Monde Café, describes it as "the coffee version of tea".

As for the $5-plus price tag for that humble long black, the Clover retails for well over $10,000.

Siphon

Once the grand dame of coffee-makers, the siphon fell out of vogue in the mid-twentieth, perhaps due to the method's complexity in comparison, say, to instant. Naturally, our coffee culture's fetish for the new — that is, the old — has revived the lost art of the siphon, and it's particular species of long, soft brewing offers a subtlety of flavour ideal for the modern panoply of beans and brands.

The siphon consists of two globes or vessels, joined by a filter and coffee. You fill the bottom one with water, and a low flame evaporates it through the coffee into the top. Remove the flame, and a gentle vacuum forms in the bottom as the steam condenses, dragging the coffeed water back through the filter.

And presto — a nuanced cup of siphoned coffee.

DUKES COFFEE ROASTERS
169 Chapel Street, Windsor

Dukes is ahead of the cafe curve in seeing coffee as the hero, not the side-kick, and embracing permutations beyond the espresso. Speaking of trends, there's also raw wood, concrete floors and stainless steel, along with knowledgeable staff and an impressive array of equipment to match their skills. A simple but well-chosen breakfast and lunch menu seals the deal.

If you're after something different, try a siphon coffee. My Kenyan estate single origin beans (the recommended choice) is prepared with a Japanese 'Hario' siphon. Made in artisanal fashion, it's one of the best ways to enjoy coffee.

The siphon-brewed coffee is a spectacular balance of natural sweetness and an initial hint of citrus, which fades almost immediately into a gentle mid-palate and crystal clean finish. Don't think you'll be disappointed with the espresso or latte; both are prepared with the same level of craftsmanship (if not the siphon theatrics). Great to see a trend-setting joint that still keeps up espresso traditions.

Phone
+613 9521 4884

Trading Hours
mon - sat: 7am - 4pm
sun: 8am - 4pm

Cafe... 23/25
Coffee... 23/25
Dukes Coffee Roasters

Inner Melbourne

CARLTON ESPRESSO
326 Lygon Street, Carlton

This modern, stylish cafe epitomises what Melburnians and visitors alike love about Lygon Street: excellent coffee, great food and genuine Italiano hospitality.

On a Saturday morning, the place is abuzz with a mixed crowd breaking fast the European way — panini stuffed with free-range eggs and pancetta or piadina (baked on-site) with all manner of fillings. I'm just here for a coffee, but the delectable range of Italian sweets by the counter proves an irresistible lure, and I succumb to the polenta and orange amaretti.

With a table, now, and my delicious 'bitter little things', the espresso arrives promptly in a sleek black cup. It gives off an exotic aroma of cardamom, and the first sip reveals a true Italian brew: spicy, strong and rich. A later flat white is even better, as the sweetness of the milk softens the edgy bitterness of the Lavazza beans. Never mind Italy — this is the authentic Lygon Street experience.

Phone
+613 9347 8482

Trading Hours
mon - sat: 7am - 9.30pm
sun: 8am - 9pm

Cafe... 21/25
Coffee... 18/25
Lavazza

PRIMARY
399 Royal Parade, Parkville

Art is big business at this ultra-modern cafe. But while the funky paintings adorning the walls are for sale, it's the coffee we're here to see – after all, owner Erin is the 2009 National Latte Art champion.

Primary is a heady mix of steel and polished concrete. However, the black ceiling and bright red accents add a bold touch to the otherwise industrial feel, while the friendly staff ensure a welcoming atmosphere. A contemporary menu offers hearty breakfasts, burgers and salads.

We score the last of the 'single origin of the day' beans. The resulting espresso is a tad weak – due to a dearth of said beans? – but has a pleasant floral aroma and bright acidity, with a short and refreshing aftertaste. The follow-up latte, made with the cafe's standard blend, is also weaker than I'd prefer. However, it's smooth and creamy with subtle chocolate undertones, and the latte art (a smiling snowman) does not disappoint. Better get in early to this one.

Phone
+613 9380 5122

Trading Hours
mon - fri: 7am - 5pm
saturday & sunday closed

Cafe... 19/25
Coffee... 18/25
Veneziano

MIXED BUSINESS
486 Queens Parade, Clifton Hill

In the seminal The Who hit, Won't Get Fooled Again, Roger Daltry and crew sing, "Meet the new boss, same as the old boss". We're quite sure they didn't have Melbourne cafe society in mind, but the line springs to mind at Clifton Hill's Mixed Business. If St Ali is the old boss of coffee south of the river, then maybe this is the new boss to the north.

It's not a coincidence that the coffee is great; after all, it is St Ali's in-house roast in use at Mixed Business. More than this, they both reside in a cool re-adaptation of an old commercial premises. Mixed Business softens this with friendly, almost family-style service, and lovely little pockets around the place where you can find a ray of sunshine to warm your skin.

An orange, sandy-coloured crema tops my espresso, with a waft of cinnamon rising from the cup. Rich berry and stone fruit flavours coat my palate, carried by a vibrant acidity. The long finish mellows leaving a bittersweet trail. Meet the new boss.

Phone
+613 9486 1606

Trading Hours
tue - sat: 7.30am - 5pm
sun: 8am - 5pm
monday closed

Cafe... 20/25
Coffee... 21/25
Seven Seeds
Specialty Coffee

BATCH ESPRESSO
Shop 1/320 Carlisle Street, Balaclava

Batch sits quietly, neighbouring a Jewish bakery: downbeat, unobtrusive and intent on making little fuss. Glass bottles along the window-bench sprout foliage that camouflages the stool-perched diners, while beats of soul and rap reverb about a black and white décor. An upturned road sign is studded with succulents, and a centrepiece of island greenery sprawls out to greet you.

Munching on some hearty fodder (black pudding, kedgeree, lamb shoulder or perhaps mountainous mash of avocado and feta), you'll notice before long a collection of Kiwi ephemera that declares owner's homeland.

Festooned with a tan version of New Zealand's silver ferns, my latte is a welcoming 'kia-ora' with a broad, wholesome profile of cashews, toasted oats and a hint of sautéed mushrooms. In the short black, there's a hazelnut aroma, buttermilk sourness and an aftertaste of lager, and its acidity hits the tongue like a stamping haka.

Phone
+613 9530 3550

Trading Hours
mon - thur: 7am - 5pm
fri: 7am - 9.30pm
sat - sun: 8am - 5pm

Cafe... 18/25
Coffee... 18/25
Coffee Supreme

Inner Melbourne

THE RUSTY DUCK
18 Margaret Street, Moonee Ponds

The Rusty Duck may be a recent addition to Moonee Ponds, but this charming little cafe is fast becoming a staple for many locals. Overlooking the train station, the cafe is a few steps away from Puckle Street — and serves some of the freshest frittatas, pizzettas and cakes in the area.

The larder behind the counter stocks everything from packet muesli to bottled jams, olives and sauces. The comfy chairs are ideal for the slow absorption of the photography adorning the walls, not to mention the chilled out background music. The staff are extremely welcoming, and meticulous detail is paid to prompt service and the cleaning of tables and plates once patrons have finished.

My espresso is sharp with a hint of salt; its aroma is flowery, with a surprising, creamy mouthfeel and flavour. By comparison, the cappuccino is alluring with a nutty aroma, its flavour a lot more elegantly rounded. Its bitterness is evened out with the right amount of sweetness.

Phone
+613 9375 2791

Trading Hours
mon - fri: 6.30am - 4.30pm
sat: 8am - 2pm
sunday closed

Cafe... 18/25
Coffee... 17/25
Vittoria

YOUNG STREET CAFE
20 Young Street, Moonee Ponds

Only the leaning umbrellas out front indicate that this old Victorian terrace is home to a cafe, and not some suburban trendites. This little cafe has a range of seating and great natural light, and as I sprawl in the rear courtyard, surrounded by vines, fruit trees and Tuscan-style furniture, it's easy to see why this is the love of the locals.

The menus are written out on paper and stuck to the walls, advertising pasta, salads and breakfast staples, as well as a huge selection of sandwiches and focaccia.

My espresso has a sweet, chocolaty smell but is sharp and intense in acidity. Its flavour is strong, the body oily and the aftertaste short and bitter in my mouth. My cappuccino is the complete paradox: mild and elegant in acidity and sweet in flavour. But it's also creamy and smooth and leaves a short, sweet aftertaste that's a real delight. Hunt down these umbrellas at once!

Trading Hours
mon - fri: 7.30am - 5pm
sat: 7.30am - 2pm
sunday closed

Cafe... 18/25
Coffee... 16/25
Genovese Coffee

Discover
Connect
Experience
Indulge

www.ama-lurra.com.au

WALL TWO80
Rear 280 Carlisle Street, Balaclava

This diminutive cafe just off bustling Carlisle Street has been around for a while now and enjoys a loyal following among locals. Unfortunately, however, even the most endearing places can be a bit hit-and-miss.

On the day of our visit, the service is somewhat surly, and my espresso arrives too hot to drink straight up. Once it cooled, the shot reveals complex earthy, tobacco and burnt toast flavours, and lingers on the tongue with a sharp, nutty aftertaste. The latte is competently made and, while it lacks personality, is pleasant enough.

Inside, a communal table and cosy nooks are perfect for the weekend papers, and the chairs on the footpath outside offer some great people-watching (there are some interesting folks around these parts). Pide dominates the menu, but we enjoy a fresh, crunchy Japanese salad of soy beans, daikon, shitake mushrooms, and sesame dressing. A bright finish after the dull start.

Phone
+613 9593 8280

Trading Hours
everyday: 6.30am - 6pm

Cafe... 14/25
Coffee... 15/25
Genovese Coffee

CAFE 3A
3a Edward Street, Brunswick

Sydney Road pulses through the north of Melbourne like an artery. A morning spent on the road can sap a traveller to leg-weariness, and the perfect tonic is Cafe 3A.

The noise abates and some kind of urban peace descends. It's a tiny little shopfront with a few seats on the footpath and an unimposing interior that further calms the jangled nerve. Normally, an out-of-date magazine rack can be cause for criticism, but somehow the eclectic array of years-old design and gossip mags makes perfect sense here. It's almost like you can engage in a little contemporary anthropology while you're nursing your cup of java.

The coffee is an Ethiopian blend, roasted locally. A lively drop, it's a low-viscosity, high-energy punch with a shortish finish and a hint of bitterness at the back of the palate. It's enjoyable and just the thing before you resurface for an afternoon in the Sydney Road shops.

Phone
+613 9380 4996

Trading Hours
mon: 8am - 4pm
wed - fri: 8am - 4pm
sat - sun: 9am - 4pm
tuesday closed

Cafe... 17/25
Coffee... 13/25
Riverside

LAWSON GROVE SHOP
1 Lawson Grove, South Yarra

This place is a hidden gem in the truest sense. Lawson Grove is a tiny cul-de-sac near the Yarra River and its eponymous cafe started off life as a communal kitchen – and only then a shop – at the bottom of some Art Deco flats designed by Melbourne architect Howard Ratcliff Lawson. These days it's mostly cafe and partly shop — selling goodies such as hand-stretched Shaw River Buffalo Mozzarella and Flip Shelton's muesli.

We take our espressos outside while enjoying the leafy neighbourhood. It's served in a shot glass, and tastes of walnut in the middle of the tongue while delivering a lemony tang at the edges. The aroma conjures freshly-baked biscuit. The follow-through is somewhat short and the texture a trifle thin, but not unpleasantly so.

The latte is creamy with a mild, caramel flavour. While locals get special treatment (a discount if you live in the street), outsiders who've made the trek are warmly welcomed and rewarded with hearty breakfast options.

Phone
+613 9866 3640

Trading Hours
mon - fri: 7.30am - 5.30pm
sat - sun: 8am - 6pm

Cafe... 18/25
Coffee... 20/25
Gravity Coffee

Inner Melbourne

SASA'S CAFE
173 Riversdale Road, Hawthorn

A visit to Sasa's is like Grandma's on a Sunday afternoon. There are floral decals on the walls, colourful vintage chairs, timber tables and Florentine cabinetry. Piles of magazines and a mess of crayons fill a wrought-iron shelf, while Mozart fills the airy space. Best of all, there are high-tea delights such as home-made date scones, passionfruit cake, brownies and pink-topped cupcakes. For the time-poor and hungry, there's also a wide selection of takeaway fare like home-made pies and moussaka.

The crowd is a little older, and most of them appear to know the owner, who exudes the graciousness and warmth of yesteryear. Meanwhile, a sign on the window boasts an award-winning barista in residence, so expectations are high. And they're not disappointed. My Genovese espresso exhibits all that is admired about Italian-style coffee... spicy aromatics, sturdy texture and a racy acidity mellowed by the combination of nuts and herbs, which stamp the palate with a long and satisfying aftertaste. A very expert Grandma indeed.

Phone
+613 9815 3885

Trading Hours
everyday: 7am - 3.30pm

Cafe... 20/25
Coffee... 18/25
Genovese Coffee

NEWTOWN SC
180 Brunswick Street, Fitzroy

In the shadows of the Atherton Gardens tower blocks, this super-cool little cafe might well have been beamed in from another planet. Newtown SC's vibe is elegantly retro: the op-shop inspired decorations are impeccably curated, with immaculate 1960s chrome, laminate and vinyl furniture. And it has for some years now been the place to be seen, especially for that particular brand of urban hipster who's too rock for the bourgeois Gertrude Street and too roll for the busy Brunswick Street further north.

Taste one of the fantastic cupcakes and you'll wonder how so many people, staff and customers alike, can look so disinterested in the presence of such fine sweets! For others, this is what inner-city living is all about — urban grit, street-smart style and a double-shot latte to go.

The coffee here is finely textured with a sweet caramel aroma, subtle nuttiness and just enough acidity to keep the flavour alive and give it a nice bright edge.

Phone
+613 9415 7337

Trading Hours
mon - fri: 8am - 4pm
sat: 9am - 4pm
sunday closed

Cafe... 18/25
Coffee... 19/25
Jasper Coffee

Photographs kindly provided by Seven Seeds

SEVEN SEEDS
106 Berkeley Street, Carlton

BEST CAFE
WINNER
DESIGN

At Seven Seeds roasting warehouse-cafe we get to smell, see and taste the experiments of coffee boffin Mark Dundon. And it's quite the mad scientist experience.

There are coffee plants on display, antique roasting machines, windows through to the cupping room, and siphon and clover coffees on offer. Converted warehouse chic heightens the funky laboratory feel — along with the excitement of knowing your beans are batch-roasted right behind that wall.

The menu is short and sleek, but it's really about the coffee. Slick little espressos of the house blend are expertly extracted to perfect each tiny cup. It's thick and viscous, wafting woody, earthy notes with a hint of pine before exploding in the mouth. A lively acidity runs across the palate, to finish with a hint of spice — and I want to hug the barista. A luscious latte to follow is more muted, but still a joy. Grab a bag to take home and maybe add a Phat Tony blend to the mix. Protective glasses sold separately.

Phone
+613 9347 8664

Trading Hours
mon - sat: 7am - 5pm
sun: 8am - 4pm

Cafe... 24/25
Coffee... 23/25

**Seven Seeds
Specialty Coffee**

PADRE
Shop 33, South Melbourne Market, South Melbourne

Buried deep within South Melbourne Market, Padre had only been open for a few months at the time of this review. However, it has already established a name (and not just the self-proclaimed 'hand-crafted coffee specialists'); armed with glistening Synesso and Mazza hardware, it has the artillery to back it up.

The shop is small, but the space is well utilised. It's evocatively lit, and has ample shelves and display cases housing coffee-related paraphernalia for sale. Aside from a few muffins and cupcakes on display, the menu is limited to coffee only, of which there's a good selection of blends and single origins.

Settling on the house 'Padre Blend', my espresso has a deep reddish-brown crema, and a vaguely nutty aroma. Rich earthy flavours, a pleasant and balanced acidity, and a long smooth finish. With the same blend, my latte loses much of the depth and richness. While beautifully made and very drinkable, I find it a little shallow when compared to my straight shot — which perhaps was too well crafted to improve on.

Phone
+613 9939 8348

Trading Hours
wed & fri: 6am - 4pm
sat - sun: 6am - 4pm
monday, tuesday & thursday closed

Cafe... 20/25
Coffee... 21/25
Padre Espresso

SMALL BLOCK
130 Lygon Street, Brunswick East

This strip of Lygon Street might be awash with some of Melbourne's hottest new cafes and restaurants, but the running sheet for the ultimate Brunswick East evening remains unchanged: 1. eat green chicken curry al fresco at Thaila Thai; 2. stroll with pistachio gelato from Gelo Bar; 3. neck an espresso at Small Block.

On weekend mornings, hordes of Brunswegians descend for nifty variations on classic dishes, such as poached eggs on cornbread with beetroot relish and fetta. Service standards are as eclectic as the Brunswick clientele, veering from friendly to aloof to MIA, especially during the breakfast rush, but it's all part of Small Block's ragged charm.

The coffee is excellent, although the house style for milk coffees tends to favour latte over caffe. The fruity aroma of the espresso announces a welcome citric tang, which is followed by a lightly earthy aftertaste that lingers on the palate.

Phone
+613 9381 2244

Trading Hours
mon - fri: 7.30am - 5pm
sat: 8am - 5pm
sun: 8.30am - 5pm

Cafe... 17/25
Coffee... 19/25
Coffee Supreme

MIDALI
261 Carlisle Street, Balaclava

Michael and David's Little espresso bar is slim and narrow but conspicuously red hot, like a Ferrari parked between white sedans. But its arresting design isn't the major attraction; that would be the live televised coverage of the action at the espresso machine, which screens all day on the plasma TV.

Tasty breakfasts are hard to concentrate on, as we watch, rapt, as sinewy arms twist, turn and tap to achieve the fine signature frond found on top of each coffee.

Espressos race to tables in white, four-cornered cups — fresh, frothy and fruity. Their swanky slick bodies surrender a zippy acidity, well-balanced flavour and crisp finish. My latte, with its musky aroma, sprints through a variety of flavours: earthy, sour and then a rush of raisin toast. All coffees leave little trace of the traction just tasted. Only vim and vigour linger.

Trading Hours
mon - fri: 7am - 6pm
sat: 8am - 5pm
sun: 8pm - 6pm

Cafe... 20/25
Coffee... 20/25
Rio Coffee

CONVENT BAKERY
1 St Heliers Street, Abbotsford

So serene is the setting that it's hard to believe the Abbotsford Convent is just four kilometres from the CBD. The former Sisters of the Good Shepherd convent is now an artists' hub that hosts farmers' and artists' markets, and is also home to one of the best-situated cafes in town: the Convent Bakery.

There are tables inside but the outdoor ones – shaded by market umbrellas and pine trees – afford a better spot to soak up the enchanting architecture. The century-old wood-fired ovens turn out fresh bread daily (and pizzas on weekends), and the range of sandwiches, cakes and biscuits is supplemented by a changing seasonal menu.

The Bakery uses its own blend of Organic Fair Trade beans (available for sale) to make an impressive coffee. My short black's spicy chocolate notes deepen into a lingering earthy taste, while the mellow, caramelly latte is more gentle, but fades quickly. If, somehow, the atmosphere doesn't keep you cloistered here for half a day, the coffee certainly will.

Phone
+613 9419 9426

Trading Hours
everyday: 7am - 5pm

Cafe... 18/25
Coffee... 17/25
Convent Bakery Blend

Photographs kindly provided by St Ali Coffee Roasters

ST ALI COFFEE ROASTERS
12 Yarra Place, South Melbourne

St Ali is to Melbourne as Mocha is to Yemen, except that this famed coffee trading spot is bustling with professionals and fashionables on their way to work. There's a fevered hubbub of coffee-questers is this warehouse tavern, mingling around the silver Synesso, sipping on a Siphon brewed drop, and with a glorious Cold Drip Filter just round the corner, you can't help but catch the contagion.

The space seems packed, but waitering dynamos manage to navigate the influx of pilgrims, and Mediterranean and Middle Eastern spices prevail from the kitchen. St Ali Nights sees the warehouse open its doors for dinner. On my visit, I devour the coconut soup with rice stock noodles, followed by twice cooked duck.

The short black is capricious and captivating. Satiny on the tongue, it's like a dervish of flavours: now sweet as muscatel, now dry as vintage white; now breathtaking in acidity, now softer with sesame. All that mellows with milk and becomes tranquil, meditative. An astonishing experience.

Phone
+613 9686 2990

Trading Hours
mon - tue: 7am - 5pm
wed - sat: 7am - 11pm
sun: 8am - 5pm

Cafe... 24/25
Coffee... 23/25

St Ali Specialty Coffee

Inner Melbourne

MART 130
107a Canterbury Road, Middle Park

Housed in a converted railway station which saw the last train rattle along to St Kilda in 1987, this cafe has a well-deserved reputation for its sumptuous breakfasts and lunches.

130 refers to the light rail stop directly out front; the terrace enjoys cooling breezes and a view of the trams sliding quietly by every so often. History buffs will enjoy poring over the old map of Melbourne and its railways that hangs on a wall inside.

We take our espresso and latte outside, looking past the light rail to the Victorian glory of the Middle Park Hotel. The espresso is burnt toast on the palate and resolves into a not unpleasant 'I smoked a cigar last night' aftertaste that hangs around. It's of medium viscosity and slightly oily. The latte is competent – certainly just the right temperature – with a soothing baked biscuit flavour; however, the crema is slightly thin and aerated, although it doesn't spoil the experience.

Phone
+613 9690 8831

Trading Hours
everyday: 7am - 3pm

Cafe... 22/25
Coffee... 18/25
Genovese Coffee

A MINOR PLACE
103 Albion Street, Brunswick East

The name is intriguing. A riff on music, birds, children? Whatever it means, neither the location nor the décor are giving it away.

Albion Street isn't the most pastoral of Brunswick locations, but the one-time milk bar is a charming abode for this busy eatery, even if it looks a little run-down from the outside. Inside, however, there's a good menu to choose from (albeit bereft of any 'minor' clues).

My coffee's crema is a rich, sandy colour and the nose is toasty with a hint of clove. The texture and flavour can't be faulted, with a long, bitter finish after a citrus and caramel dose.

If a complaint could be raised, it'd be the slightly sniffy service. But maybe in this post-modern world of the gritty über-cool, that's not an accident.

Phone
+613 9384 3131

Trading Hours
mon - sat: 8am - 5pm
sun: 8.30am - 5pm

Cafe... 16/25
Coffee... 19/25
Atomica

SOCIAL ROASTING COMPANY
307 Racecource Road, Flemington

From the ashes of former tenant Octane Espresso, rises a new breed of cafe with less, well, octane and more social conscience: the Social Roasting Company. Freshly roasted coffee comes from their Flemington Roastery, where the head roaster got his hands on a German Probat machine and some fair trade beans.

They're also trying to reduce their carbon footprint by making deliveries using peddle power. This may take a little longer than normal, but thankfully my coffee order is promptly filled.

My espresso is served up by a chatty barista who informs me I'm drinking their Social Blend, no less. Perfect length and temperature, with a dark chocolate coloured crema, it has a velvety mouthfeel and complex finish. Advertised on a black chalked wall is the full range of freshly roasted coffee, and both my conscience and my palate force me to buy a bag of beans. A delivery from Flemington would take too long…

Phone
+613 9372 3288

Trading Hours
mon - fri: 7am - 4pm
sat - sun: 8am - 4pm

Cafe... 19/25
Coffee... 21/25

Social Roasting Company

Inner Melbourne

THE FIRST POUR
26 Bond Street, Abbotsford

Cars with a lot of grunt dominate the street parking, and the aroma of malt and hops muster in the air. The Veneziano warehouse roastery stands out from its neighbouring breweries with a signature livery of yellow and black, and inside you'll find the First Pour cafe — along with animated businessmen and coffee-connoisseurs dissecting the flavour profile of the day's blend.

Hessian sacks are stretched to fit light fixtures, and the wallpaper of yellow and orange with liquid black designs is almost hallucinogenic. And then you spot the bright La Marzocco — the caffeine world's equivalent of a yellow Lamborghini.

My Bella Vita blend espresso has a leathery biscotti aroma, sour clove savour and tart, sucking acidity. The blend masters the milk in a latte to keep on kicking, while the milk in turn revives some of the espresso's dark chocolate flavours and sustains a roasted richness from first pour to final drop.

Phone
+613 9421 5585

Trading Hours
mon - fri: 8am - 5pm
sat: 9am - 1pm
sunday closed

Cafe... 19/25
Coffee... 21/25
Veneziano

ARCADIA
193 Gertrude Street, Fitzroy

Peddling into Fitzroy, I could sense the change in the air. The wheels of progress have gained momentum in the past few years, attracting big name chefs – like Andrew McConnell of Cutler & Co. – as well as fashion brands, all claiming their stake of groovy Gertrude St. Among it all (and opposite Industria by Max Watts), lies Arcadia.

This cafe has been around longer than most, and continues to lure its fair share of Fitzroy punters for coffee and lazy lunch. And as the strip evolves and changes, so has Arcadia's coffee supplier. They've recently introduced Toby's Estate Fair Trade coffee (timed, coincidentally, with Toby's migration from Sydney to the real home of Australian coffee).

So I order a coffee roasted by the new kids in town — an espresso, with good length, a slight floral aroma and great temperature. It has a syrupy mouthfeel, intense spice characters and a tangy finish on the back palate. I wash it all down with a fresh juice combination, and head out to the sunny courtyard to enjoy the fresh winds of change.

Phone
+613 9416 1055

Trading Hours
mon - fri: 8am - 5pm
sat - sun: 9am - 5pm

Cafe... 17/25
Coffee... 15/25
Toby's Estate

DI BELLA ROASTING WAREHOUSE
19 Leveson Street, North Melbourne

Inner Melbourne

This bright and breezy, warehouse-style space in historic North Melbourne operates as a roastery and laid-back cafe that's ideal for weekend brunching. Bring along your biggest and best appetite – or hangover – for the sizzling clay pot of cevapcici, smoky bacon, eggs, mushies, tomatoes, and house-made baked beans. Then restart your nervous system with a Di Bella espresso.

Mine is tangy and sharp, and loiters for a while on the palate before softening into Brazil nut and toffee flavours. A clean, grit-free brew, it boasts rich viscosity and feels clean in the mouth, with aromas of tobacco and spice. The latte chaser has a comforting, bready aroma and is well rounded with a biscuity flavour.

There are wines available by the glass (should brunch turn into an all-afternoon affair), but note that the kitchen closes at three. These guys love spreading the word about the bean and, as such, conduct regular coffee appreciation classes for small groups.

Phone
+613 9329 2973

Trading Hours
mon - fri: 7am - 5pm
sat - sun: 7.30am - 4pm

Cafe... 20/25
Coffee... 22/25
Di Bella Coffee

NINETEEN SQUARES CAFE
31 Blessington Street, St Kilda

This miniature treasure trove's 19 square metres of bohemian charm spill out onto a leafy street strewn with random tables, chairs, stools and the odd milk crate or six. This little gem has a vein of gold running through its eclectic heart.

There's a warm, everyone-knows-everyone vibe set to the chill sounds of Damien Rice. Add a quirky touch, including rows of collectors' teaspoons (not for sale) and brightly coloured, reusable KeepCups (for sale). Toss in a small but appealing menu, featuring eggs poached in a terracotta pot with chorizo or grilled veg, and a World-Famous Chicken Sanga. Finish with a shot of Coffee Supreme's Fair Trade Organic, and you're on a winning streak.

My espresso is rich and earthy, yet elegant — a dance of finely-balanced bitter-sweetness on the tongue and a lingering spiced-chocolate finish. After a chat with the well-informed barista, there's a creamy cappuccino to follow, creatively topped with chocolate shavings. Pure gold.

Phone
+613 8598 9919

Trading Hours
mon - fri: 6.30am - 5pm
sat - sun: 7am - 5pm

Cafe... 20/25
Coffee... 22/25
Coffee Supreme

NOT ALL THERE
194 Wells Street, South Melbourne

Despite being hidden away and hemmed in by high-rises, this laid-back cafe is fast becoming the area's favourite haunt.

And it's easy to see why. The cosy den-like surroundings are complemented by super-friendly staff and a comfort-food menu (think ready-made panini, thick-cut raisin toast and mains like salmon risotto or slow-cooked beef on mash).

It's also a great place for a caffeine fix, as the queue of punters proves. Despite the crush, there's no rushing; each coffee is made with care by a barista who obviously loves his job. Unsurprisingly, it's superb. The herbal aroma of my espresso gives way to a complex wine-like brew: tart and thick on the tongue, with a pleasantly strong acidity and long finish. With milk, the flavour is similarly robust but somewhat sweeter (although this could be the surprise chocolate centre of my accompanying raspberry muffin).

Not all there? On the contrary — this place has it in spades.

Phone
+613 9078 1298

Trading Hours
mon - fri: 7am - 4pm
saturday & sunday closed

Cafe... 19/25
Coffee... 21/25
Veneziano

YOUR SLAYER AWAITS

✶ ✶ ✶ ✶ ✶

Enquiries,
orders, metal lust

✶ ✶ ✶ ✶ ✶

Coffee Supreme,
Melbourne

03 9428 3148

Logos,
brands, trademarks

✶ ✶ ✶ ✶ ✶

SLAYER

Coffee Supreme

PHOTOGRAPHER: ALEX ASLANGUL

Coffee Supreme in Australia was born out of lessons learnt while Justin Emerson was working in the New Zealand company of the same name. In 2001, Marsha Partington and Justin moved to Melbourne from Wellington, as – like hundreds of Kiwis at the time – they were unable to resist the pull of the "*big* big city."

While doing his time behind (and under) numerous coffee machines, Justin came to the conclusion that what Melbourne needed was 1) the coffee; and 2) the service that he was accustomed to giving back in the homeland.

So from humble beginnings around mid-2002, Coffee Supreme Australia was born. We found a small warehouse in the back blocks of Cremorne, and Justin convinced Marsha to roast after hours. It was about providing an alternative to the prevailing coffees of indeterminate age and dubious origin, supplied with no support to baristas and cafes.

Surprisingly, there were businesses willing to take a risk on a couple of kids from NZ; the likes of Ray Cafe, Tre Bicchieri, Le Chien and Batch Espresso spread the word that there were good coffee, good people and great service to be found about town.

Coffee Supreme is one of the few companies out there that can offer a solution for everything a cafe comes up against, all from under the one roof. The coffee beans are sourced and roasted with care (believe it or not — exceptional green coffee is becoming easier to find, and it's a given here at Coffee Supreme that their roasted coffees are good).

" **At Coffee Supreme, we pride ourselves on our service. Our beans get people's attention, but it's the quality of our staff that keeps people coming back.** "

Little by little, the demand grew until they were running there little GN12 Probat roaster almost around the clock.

Nowadays, the G60 Probat takes pride of place in the previously abandoned mechanics workshop of the Phoenix biscuit factory, but little else has changed: it's all about delivering stellar coffee, with the service and support to back it up.

"We like to think it's not all about the toys, bells and whistles. Granted, quality equipment is essential; however, the people behind the scenes, the people feeding, fixing, running, growing and supporting everything are far more important to us than the size of your roaster, or the label your espresso machine sports, or the far-flung reaches of the world where your green coffee comes from. For the cafe owner, quality people are the key," Justin says.

Trusted espresso machinery — whether it be a San Marco, Slayer, Synesso or La Marzocco — is well cared for by their technical team; with a maintenance plan offering peace of mind that the machines will be looked after. Espresso training is provided for all their customers: running an in-house training program where baristas can learn the basics or refine latte art skills.

Justin goes on to add, "and we're all about deliveries, service and support. When you run out of beans at five to eight on Monday morning, all you want to hear is, 'We'll be there in ten!' We can do that for Melbourne businesses — in fact, we hand-deliver all our local coffee. But out of town cafes are also serviced by our courier company — which we keep on a pretty tight leash, so it's rare that anyone goes wanting."

Coffee Supreme

Chris, Jona or Justin are there to talk you through anything cafe-related — from numbers, margins and profitability to the most efficient way to set up your space, staff hiring and ergonomics.

When it comes to helping out cafe owners, Justin points out, "one of the most common things we see in new cafe set-ups are compromises made to the way the bar is designed. Efficiency is key here, along with space, ergonomics and refrigeration. Nothing slows down drink construction like a lack of bench space." As a cafe grows, the rest of the team gets involved, with Ange, Betty and Ben handling orders, and Adrian and Hayden at the ready for machine tune-ups - or if one of its wheels falls off (which is pretty rare, considering all equipment is loaded into a database and serviced every three months). Coffee Supreme gets all these back-of-house things right, so we can sit back and enjoy the brew.

" To all our customers, suppliers and supporters, past and present, thanks for choosing us, we hope you enjoy the show, "

Justin Emerson

PICCOLO ESPRESSO
149 High Street, Prahran

The street directory will tell you that this little gem resides in Prahran, but in its heart and soul it resonates with the decidedly more authentic vibe of neighbouring Windsor. An energetic young crew echoes the sentiment, and there are laidback beats and old-fashioned warmth.

The coffee is from Kiwi-cum-Aussie operation, Coffee Supreme, and it's a surprising cup. A nice rush of berries on the palate before it settles into a real shortbread-and-chocolate length. It has a lovely mouthfeel and a good oily viscosity. It's well-prepared and impressive.

Equally impressive are the hours these guys keep, finishing in the wee-smalls three nights a week, with live music, DJs and a licensed bar to wend through the night. Proximity to Swinburne University means a healthy supply of regulars during the day, and a music program that distinguishes them from the usual Prahran homogeneity ensures a night-time following.

Phone
+613 9521 4306

Trading Hours
mon - thur: 7am - 10pm
fri: 7am - 1am
sat - sun: 8am - 1am

Cafe... 17/25
Coffee... 20/25
Coffee Supreme

ESPRESSO 3121
Rear 96 Balmain Street, Richmond

Espresso 3121 occupies an airy warehouse space up a laneway in Cremorne — a history-laden mini-suburb of Richmond which lies in the shadows of the old Bryant and May match factory. Vaguely filling the space are huge communal tables and smaller ones near the open windows.

An enormous blackboard menu lists the usual suspects – stuff on toast, or toasted sandwiches – and my HTC is excellent. Also on offer is avocado and vegemite on toast, which prove strange but delicious bedfellows.

Coffee, however, is the thing, as the long Java menu attests. My espresso, a single-origin Nicaraguan, is rich and sweet with tangy, citrus hints. Smooth and well-rounded, it resolves on the palate into a lovely, burnt lemon zest. The latte is a little less inspiring: the crema is thin and the temperature a trifle hot. It lacks kick, after the espresso, and requires cheering up with some sugar.

Phone
+613 9025 7620

Trading Hours
mon - fri: 7am - 4pm
saturday & sunday closed

Cafe... 20/25
Coffee... 20/25
Veneziano

FRATELLI
300 Clarendon Street, South Melbourne

This cafe/bar/restaurant offers something for everyone, whether it's an early-morning caffeine shot or a late nightcap. Big bi-fold doors open the spacious, red-brick room onto Clarendon Street, with an old-fashioned verandah providing shade — and shelter from tram noise. Generously spaced tables, including a communal table, offer room for prams and quiet corners for business meetings, while there's also plenty of seating outside.

The back-corner kitchen is kept busy with an expansive menu that includes breakfast, lunch, dinner and drinks; however, those seeking only a coffee are just as welcome.

My espresso has a golden-caramel crema and a nice interplay between unsweetened cocoa and wood. Intense and viscous, it enjoys a long, sweet aftertaste. The latte has an unusually strong flavour, its nutty caffeine taste almost overpowering the milk. While intense, it's not at all unpleasant — and perhaps the perfect chaser to a few drinks.

Phone
+613 9690 6322

Trading Hours
tue - sat: 7am - 9pm
sun - mon: 7am - 6pm

Cafe... 17/25
Coffee... 17/25
Di Bella Coffee

APPETITE CAFE
8 Errol Street, North Melbourne

Errol Street's scruffy appeal is mirrored in the ethos of Appetite Cafe. The green and white floor tiles date from some mysterious, prior occupancy; the pockmarked walls have been unceremoniously painted in pale green; and the furniture isn't meant to be much more than tidy.

The menu looks straightforward too – the requisite big breakfast, hearty home-style pies and a range of melts – but despite this unassuming image, Appetite hits the mark where it matters most. They roast their own coffee (and sell beans for home). And those melts! The tuna example is studded with salty capers and olives, and sweetened up with a hint of red onion.

The house blend is extracted with a thin, tan crema, but the light-bodied espresso has real staying power, with fresh, peppery spice notes that invite a second cup.

Phone
+613 9328 4582

Trading Hours
wed - mon: 6am - 5pm
tuesday closed

Cafe... 15/25
Coffee... 15/25
Appetite Blend

DEAD MAN ESPRESSO
35 Market Street, South Melbourne

Few cafes take coffee as seriously – and do it as well – as Dead Man Espresso. With coffee from Seven Seeds (including a special house blend) and single origin beans from other Melbourne roasters, a lot of thought has gone into the cup. Then there's the serious, modern look of clean lines, timber tables and an impressive balcony area, along with a small but thoughtful menu.

A Synesso machine takes pride of place at the serving area, while the pour over coffee equipment adds a theatrical touch. An inky espresso tastes of unsweetened cocoa and delivers a mouth punch of flavour. It's intense but balanced and a delight to drink. My latte is creamily elegant, with harmonious flavours playing on the palate.

The pour over, an Ethiopian Beloya blend, smacks of aniseed and blueberry; less intense than an espresso, it's full of flavour but gentle on the palate — and a great exponent of a growing trend.

Phone
+613 9686 2255

Trading Hours
mon - fri: 7am - 4pm
sat - sun: 8am - 4pm

Cafe... 21/25
Coffee... 22/25

Seven Seeds & Featured Specialty Roasters

Inner Melbourne

detox your coffee machine...

Cino Cleano espresso machine cleaning products help to:

- ✸ clean away impurities and remove scale
- ✸ keep your espresso machine in top condition
- ✸ produce fresh tasting coffee every time

 **espresso machine cleaning solution**

 **espresso machine backflush cleaner**

 **espresso machine liquid descaler**

 **espresso machine cleaning tablets**

 **milk frother cleaner**

Cleaning products and accessories for every small office or domestic coffee machine.

...and accessories to
help make you
the expert barista

www.cinocleano.com

visit **www.cinocleano.com**
call **1300 364 440** or
email us at **enquiry@cinocleano.com**

LUNCHEONETTE
173 Rankins Road, Kensington

Frank Sinatra sang it best: "If I can make it there, I'll make it anywhere, New York." Olivia Robinson has done just that, working in The Big Apple's coolest cafes and returning home with the idea for Luncheonette.

The place feels like a tiny diner cafe on the Lower East Side: unpolished but not gritty, and adorned with a few second-hand pieces (a working vintage cash register takes centre stage).

To one side is a two-group La San Marco coffee machine, which pumps out Coffee Supreme's Organic Fair Trade blend. My espresso is at a good temperature, and has a spicy, fruity aroma; dark chocolate and sharp acidity, with a short finish. It's a little gritty, but well balanced overall.

A clever use of space allows a tiny kitchen to put together some simple but winning combinations. Baked eggs with pancetta, or tomato, buffalo mozzarella and pesto sandwiched by Dench Bread. Start spreading the news...

Trading Hours
tue - sun: 8am - 3pm
monday closed

Cafe... 18/25
Coffee... 17/25
Coffee Supreme

DUNDAS PLACE CAFE
131 Dundas Place, Albert Park

For a cafe to survive in competition-heavy Albert Park, it has to deliver the goods. At Dundas Place Cafe, this is done through the trifecta of great food, great coffee and great service — and the punters are packing in, even on a miserable Melbourne morning.

Sensing our need for caffeine, the cheery waiter takes our coffee order before leaving us to contemplate the breakfast menu. There's plenty to choose from: old favourites rub shoulders with more modern dishes such as Smoked Salmon and Corn Cakes, or Asparagus and Prosciutto, while the counter is awash with muffins, cookies and cakes.

The espresso arrives quickly and provides a welcome pick-me-up. It's a nippy brew with a strong floral aroma and rich caramel crema. Thick on the tongue, with medium acidity, it delivers a short, sharp aftertaste. The addition of milk brings out the sweetness, rounding out the acidity and creating a mild, extremely drinkable latte. We could stay here all day.

Phone
+613 9699 4561

Trading Hours
everyday: 7am - 5pm

Cafe... 19/25
Coffee... 20/25
Atomica

AUCTION ROOMS
103 Errol Street, North Melbourne

This former auction house on Errol Street has been stripped back to bare brick and transformed into one of the freshest, brightest, most inviting coffee venues you're likely to visit. Melbourne architects Six Degrees have a talent for combining the rustic with the resolutely modern, and this place is no exception. There's an abandoned-factory feel, as walls have been knocked out and nature is just starting to take over. Sunlight streams in through a long strip of skylights onto unvarnished, honey-toned floorboards; a wall of glass looks over a courtyard shaded by olive trees; and at the centre of the room, a slick island bar is a hive of activity.

And yet, despite all this fuss over the architecture, coffee is undeniably king here. They roast their own, and a rotating single-origin special is always on offer, along with the wonderfully multicultural blend of four beans, sourced from Ethiopia, Sumatra, Guatemala and El Salvador. This makes for a wonderfully creamy, chocolate espresso which leaves a delightfully rich, stewed-fruit aftertaste. Sold!

Phone
+613 9326 7749

Trading Hours
mon - wed: 7.30am - 4pm
thur - fri: 7.30am - 10pm
sat: 8am - 10pm
sun: 8am - 4pm

Cafe... 22/25
Coffee... 22/25
Small Batch

Inner Melbourne

CHIMMY'S
342 Bridge Road, Richmond

Forget the tonnes of stainless steel and acres of polished concrete floors that epitomise the Bridge Road cafe scene. Chimmy's is more of a country bakery that's been plonked in the middle of Richmond with its stereo set to funky Spanish flamenco.

The staff are professional, if a little standoffish, however, the lack of table service can present issues. Being on my own and having finished my espresso, I go to the counter to order a latte, only to find my seat occupied when I return to my table. The food overshadows these minor foibles though. There's a wide selection of flaky pastries, pide and Turkish bread. Delectable sweets are on display behind glass, and fresh breads fill the front window.

My espresso has a light brown crema, licking up the sides of the demitasse, and a bready aroma. A medium acidity with strong rear palate and a long chocolaty finish. My latte is pleasingly mild and quaffable.

Phone
+613 9427 1391

Trading Hours
everyday: 6am - 9pm

Cafe... 18/25
Coffee... 17/25
Melba Coffee

LEROY ESPRESSO
191 Acland Street, St Kilda

This St Kilda staple is perched right on the corner of Acland Street, but Leroy doesn't rest on its premier location. After all, there's plenty of competition along the strip. There's something of a retro vibe in the orange and brown tones, yet little about it feels dated. Weekend breakfasts keep locals coming back – and lure newcomers in – with temptations like the fluffy stacks of pancakes, best enjoyed street-side so you can gloat in full view.

It's even better when it arrives hand-in-hand with a thick and oily espresso. Powerful and potent in its tiny little cup, this coffee mouthful packs a punch up front, with a light, bright acidity leaving a hint of citrus in its wake. The creamy latte that follows is on the milky side, but it's velvety smooth and mellow.

Take note of the sign by the bar reading "Prices may vary with customer attitude"; we assume it's a joke, because the coffee has 'tude enough for anybody.

Phone
+613 9525 5166

Trading Hours
mon - fri: 7am - 5pm
sat - sun: 7am - 6pm

Cafe... 19/25
Coffee... 19/25
Merlo Coffee

GROWERS ESPRESSO
332 St Georges Road, Fitzroy North

Head north, away from the perennially hip Brunswick Street strip, and you'll bump into a decidedly less self-conscious quarter near what was once the Aberdeen Hotel. In an old shop-front on the corner is Growers Espresso, a cafe that acts as a retail outlet for Eureka Coffee, representing predominantly Australian coffee growers from northern NSW and northern Queensland.

The proprietors wear their heart on their sleeve, with Fairtrade and Direct Trade varieties on offer, and on any given day you'll find special blends or single estate brews.

The beans are roasted onsite and the espresso is a lovely, earthy choc-fruit affair, full of plum and cherry notes, with good, toffee viscosity. Enjoy your brew in the small, naturally light, welcoming space, or take it on the run as the Number 112 tram flits by. Light snacks like toasted sandwiches and biscuits are also available from the counter, but the pervading mood is one of passion for the coffee. You can't ask for much more than that.

Phone
+613 9486 1886

Trading Hours
mon - sat: 8am - 3pm
sunday closed

Cafe... 18/25
Coffee... 20/25
Eureka Coffee

ATOMICA
268 Brunswick Street, Fitzroy

The mushroom cloud of coffee-bean smoke that emanates from within Atomica has, like a caffeine-spiked siren's call, tempted many a Fitzroy resident to its door. Behind that door, the cafe itself is rather pokey and dark, truth be told, and out front, the tables and seats along the footpath might've been stolen from a primary school. But none of that matters — this place is a Fitzroy classic; the coffee is always high quality, the atmosphere intimate; and we'll be damned if we prise ourselves out from behind our tiny al fresco table until we're good and ready to go!

Bean spotters, however, plump for a spot next to the grand old coffee roaster at the back of the cafe, where they can watch the beans darken while toying with the options on the coffee menu. The default house blend is lovingly extracted in a palate-coating, full-bodied espresso with a hint of molasses sweetening the nose. It has strong roasted-nut flavours and great acidity for a refreshing finish. Seriously good coffee.

Phone
+613 9417 4255

Trading Hours
mon - fri: 7.30am - 5.30pm
sat - sun: 8.30am - 5.30pm

Cafe... 19/25
Coffee... 21/25
Atomica

BRAZIL LIFESTYLE CAFE
111 Cecil Street, South Melbourne

At first glance, it seems there's not much the folks at BLC don't know about coffee. From the retro-inspired Diedrich roaster in the window to the range of blends, single origins and coffee-making paraphernalia that line the shelves, there's something for every caficionado. Even the walls are in on the act, with posters outlining the finer points of blending, cupping and extracting the perfect brew.

Unfortunately, this knowledge doesn't always translate into practice. Our first visit yields a pale, under-extracted espresso and a scalding latte, both of which disappoint in the flavour stakes. However, a different day and a different barista result in a different story. This time, the pleasant herby aroma of an espresso gives way to complex winey undertones with just the right amount of acidity and oiliness on the tongue. The latte is similarly well prepared, the milk rounding out the tang.

The verdict? Definitely worth a visit, but pick your day – and your barista – carefully.

Phone
+613 9077 8094

Trading Hours
mon - fri: 7am - 5pm
sat: 7.30am - 5pm
sun: 8am - 5pm

Cafe... 18/25
Coffee... 17/25
Brazil Lifestyle

PROUD MARY
172 Oxford Street, Collingwood

WINNER BEYOND THE CALL OF DUTY
RUNNER UP BEST BREAKFAST
RUNNER UP GOD SHOT

Inner Melbourne

Quite who Mary is isn't especially apparent, but the pride is everywhere in evidence. The converted-warehouse cafe has all the exposed brick and polished concrete we know and love, yet here, in an urban-industrial first, it's warm, human and homey. Like an urban-industrial breakfast nook. Much of this belongs to the service — a waitress offers us real cutlery to take away when a disposable set isn't immediately found. Tina Turner mid power ballad doesn't summon such genuine energy. (Our apologies if 'Proud Mary' is not in fact a Mrs T reference.)

A lively menu struggles not to be overshadowed by the coffee, with Spanish-accented hits such as the Pork Belly Sandwich with smoked paprika relish and aioli. ¡Hola! But yes, in the end, the coffee steals the show — and not only because of the spanking blue six group Synesso, as well as a swag of grinders and syphons. The Brazilian sambas into a macchiato, and a nimble sweetness dances on the palate with flourishes of lime and a sultry acidity. The length of the shot – which definitely has legs – is matched by headpiece of delicately structured milk. Take a bow, Mary, wherever you are.

Phone
+613 9417 5930

Trading Hours
mon - fri: 7am - 4pm
sat - sun: 8am - 4pm

Cafe... 24/25
Coffee... 24/25

5 Senses Coffee & Proud Mary Origins

BABKA BAKERY CAFE
358 Brunswick Street, Fitzroy

Good things do come to those who wait in the notoriously long queue at this gem of a cafe. It's also a pleasant wait amid the wooden furniture, eclectic fixtures and a bakery that's as popular as the cafe. There's a distinct Russian theme to the menu, their signature dish being Maroussia's Pan Fried Dumplings — filled with potato and mushroom and served with dill and sour cream. You can whet your appetite with a Kousmichoff Smoky Samovar tea, or a coffee.

According to the ballerina-like waitress, who seems to glide across the floor to a symphony of rattling cutlery and crockery, they use a local grind known as Romeo. The elements of the espresso are like the layers of a Babushka doll: a uniquely caramel aroma followed by vibrant acidity; a luxuriously sweet body and teasingly short aftertaste which leaves me wanting more.

While pramsters may not agree (a sign reads "Prams too big — Babka only little"), the rest of us will doubtless be returning to this little Russia, with love.

Phone
+613 9416 0091

Trading Hours
tue - sun: 7am - 7pm
monday closed

Cafe... 17/25
Coffee... 20/25
Caffe Romeo

SPOONFUL
543 High Street, Prahran

Judging by the general hubbub and the multi-generational groups chatting around communal tables, this joint is a hit with locals. The French country-kitchen ambience is conducive to a long weekend lunch, and the menu boasts enticing dishes such as Pad Thai Omelette with Chilli Rock Sugar. If there's just two of you, enjoy a tête-a-tête and a cuppa in a cosy corner.

My espresso is a trifle thin and could do with more complexity, but I'm enjoying its liquorice and burnt toffee flavours. It's short on finish but feels clean and refreshing in the mouth. I also try a well-executed latte which has cocoa characteristics and a pleasant nutty aroma. The crema is excellent. Put this place on your weekend to-do list, and check out the giant Chinese lanterns hanging above the kitchen, too.

Sino-Francophiles will have a ball.

Phone
+613 9521 5212

Trading Hours
mon - sat: 7.30am - 4.30pm
sun: 8am - 4pm

Cafe... 18/25
Coffee... 17/25
Genovese

NABIHA
10 Hall Street, Moonee Ponds

Melbourne's West has an unfortunate reputation as a bit of a coffee wasteland. Until, that is, you stumble upon Nabiha. Named for the owners' late aunt, the Breathe Architecture-designed space feels like a modern espresso bar off a cobbled city laneway, with clean lines, recycled-timber floors, bare concrete walls and modern white tables. They managed to squeeze in a tiny kitchen, which turns out simple, tasty food inspired by the owners' Italian and Middle Eastern heritage.

At the time of our review, Nabiha has only been open for a couple of weeks — but the coffee is already a standout. Perhaps this is to be expected, what with a barista from Proud Mary, a sparkly three-group Synesso machine and a blend crafted by 5 Senses. My espresso has an earthy sweet nose, chocolaty characteristics and a velvety mouthfeel with mild acidity. So good I have to grab another.

With soulful James Brown tunes by playing in the background, I leave thinking the West deserves more places like this. Auntie Nabiha would be proud.

Trading Hours
mon - fri: 8am to 4pm
sat - sun: 9am to 3pm

Cafe... 20/25
Coffee... 21/25
5 Senses Coffee

Now serving in Melbourne

*R*aising the espresso bar

Campos

Specialty Coffee Professionals
www.camposcoffee.com

MIN LOKAL
422 George Street, Fitzroy

Locals might mourn the loss of artisan bakery Wild Flour, but the best way to get over an old flame is in the arms of a new one. To wit, Min Lokal moved in and Fitzroy was in love again.

Aesthetically, not much has changed: the cumbersome baker's oven made way for a display case loaded with cakes, a second communal table and a few nick-nacks. The floor staff are impeccably cool – think oversized '80s glasses, manicured moustaches and sprayed-on jeans – but also super friendly and highly functioning, wheeling out homestyle sandwiches and other morsels with the efficiency of a Casio calculator watch.

This stretch of George Street is leafy and tranquil, and the streetside tables offer a wonderful spot for lingering over an afternoon latte. The coffee here matches the mood. Its dense ginger crema and viscous extraction offer an elegant balance of mild acidity and a nutty aftertaste. No harsh extremes, just caffeine and comfort food.

Phone
+613 9417 0333

Trading Hours
mon - fri: 7am - 4pm
sat - sun: 8.30am - 4pm

Cafe... 18/25
Coffee... 19/25
Coffee Supreme

7 GRAMS
505 Church Street, Richmond

All it takes is seven grams to extract a rich espresso shot. And all it takes is a lead foot to zoom by and miss this express pit-stop. It's not a milkbar, though its shopfront is as small. It's simply everything you want for a day on the go. Staff with a smile and service with speed. Tables stretch along the street for those with time to linger, while a mirror inside runs the length of a bench with vinyl stools, its reflection deliciously doubling each order.

The espresso is loaded, pungent, as sweetly sour as a green-skin grape. The aftertaste is tart and pronounced. The latte, with its lathered milk, is like sliding the senses into cruise control. Its scent is softer and more rounded, its flavour of walnut is stylishly smooth, with a swerving acidity to enliven the palate.

All it takes is seven grams, well tamped, to re-charge any day.

Phone
+613 9429 8505

Trading Hours
mon - fri: 6am - 4pm
saturday & sunday closed

Cafe... 18/25
Coffee... 16/25
Veneziano

LIAR LIAR
90 Kincora Street, Hawthorn

'Big Iron' espresso equipment dominates Liar Liar's counter space, and a blackboard behind it soberly states the single origin coffees available. Even the door knob, a group-handle from an espresso machine, hints that Liar Liar has gone to great lengths to pay homage to the bean.

With its austere modern décor, the cafe is packed with patrons, though at no time do I feel rushed. Friendly and professional staff work like a well-oiled machine.

The menu has a range of regular breakfast and lunch options, and a supplementary coffee menu offers rarer selections, such as three variations of macchiato and a piccolo. Fresh juices abound, with playful names such as Golden Pash, Purple Sunrise and Hippy Juice.

My Brazil Fazenda espresso arrives with a light brown crema and nutty aroma. Expertly extracted, it's bright, punchy, and has a clean, short finish. The Ethiopian Yirgacheffe has a flowery aroma, syrupy sweetness and fruit acidity that gives way to a wonderfully smooth finish. An exceptional experience.

Inner Melbourne

Phone
+613 9818 8864

Trading Hours
mon - fri: 7am - 5pm
sat - sun: 8am - 5pm

Cafe... 22/25
Coffee... 23/25

**Sensory Lab &
5 Senses Coffee**

THE COFFEE COMPANY
260 Carlisle Street, Balaclava

This gourmet roastery might've been around for four decades, but patrons still arrive with a twinkle in their eye to ask for their weekly supplies. As you enter, baskets of loose, bronzed beans make it hard to resist plunging your hands in to scoop up a faceful of aromatic hedonism.

The shelves are laden with strainers, glasses, ibriks and plungers; loose-leaf teas, nuts and imported schokolades (hot chocolate). Green beans wait their turn in the roaster, which sweats in the front window and fills the space with a warm, buttery aroma.

The house blend, always Java Express, arrives short and black and scented like butterscotch with a crema to match. It's as light on the tongue as an anisette, tangy and piquant like lemon tart. The latte is endlessly quaffable; its mild nuttiness comforts and consoles, and a peppery note wafts with smoky tobacco — or perhaps that's the glamorous Marlene Dietrich postered nearby.

Phone
+613 9534 6604

Trading Hours
mon - fri: 8.30am - 6pm
sat: 8.30am - 5pm
sunday closed

Cafe... 17/25
Coffee... 18/25
The Coffee Company

BRUNETTI
194 Faraday Street, Carlton

The word 'institution' is often bandied about, to the point where its distinction has waned. But if we can revive the term for a minute – perhaps with the aid of an espresso hit – then Brunetti's is every bit Melbourne's original coffee institution.

Its pedigree is as Italian as Lygon Street itself, and at busy times it can look like Sienna's Piazza del Campo — such are the crowds. The interior is a cool interpretation of contemporary European chic; the staff is efficient, if sometimes a little harried.

The espresso has a punchy, nutty nose and a chocolate-coated-cranberry profile that wafts away to a nicely bitter but not inaccessible finish. If you're looking to escape the crowds, Brunetti probably isn't the place, but if you're after a little bit of Italian flair with your latte, then you know how this ends…

Phone
+613 9347 2801

Trading Hours
sun - thur: 6am - 11pm
fri - sat: 6am - midnight

Cafe... 16/25
Coffee... 14/25
Brunetti Blend

Main Photograph By Victor Pugatschew.
Kindly provided by Three Bags Full

THREE BAGS FULL
Shop 3/46 Nicholson Street, Abbotsford

Knowing this cafe is the newest venture by the team behind APTE and Liar Liar, I'm three bags full of expectation. The cafe, housed in an old hat factory, projects industrial chic, with stools made from old road signs, antique scales holding cupcakes, and inverted coffee cups and saucers used as light fittings.

I visit on a Saturday morning and although the place seems full to capacity, the attentive waitstaff find me the last seat in the house, which happens to be right behind the gleaming chrome Synesso and its duo of baristas. A blackboard announces the two signature espresso blends and single origin blends on offer for espresso, pour over and Clover methods.

My signature blend espresso has a honey-coloured crema and complex herbaceous aroma. Liquorice and herbs strike the palate, and the mouthfeel is lusciously buttery, ending in a divine combination of dark chocolate and wild berries. My single origin (Columbian) flat white is equally exquisite. Expectations are more than met.

Phone
+613 9421 2732

Trading Hours
mon - fri: 7am - 4pm
sat - sun: 8am - 4pm

Cafe... 24/25
Coffee... 23/25
5 Senses Coffee

OUTPOST BY ST ALI
9 Yarra Street, South Yarra

This cafe is literally an outpost of St Ali, the legendary South Melbourne-based purveyor of fine coffee well known to readers of this guide. Nestled in the ground floor of a new residential development, the place looks like a country kitchen — and isn't much bigger than one, either.

The chefs here rustle up a fine breakfast (try the fresh-cut papaya with lemon, pomegranate and yoghurt) or a hearty lunch (the menu boasts slow-roasted pork belly, among other delights). And then, of course, there's the famous St Ali coffee.

My espresso is complex and rounded, with bold, spicy flavours giving way to a nutty sweetness on the palate; it's rich and slightly oily with a nutmeg aroma. The latte is pure St Ali, with a perfect body and soothing baked-bread aroma. It has a smooth, robust consistency and is nutty and sweet to taste — no sugar needed. Outpost has already become a firm favourite with the demanding denizens of 3141; now for *The Coffee Guide* crowd.

Phone
+613 9827 8588

Trading Hours
mon - fri: 7am - 5pm
sat - sun: 8am - 4pm

Cafe... 19/25
Coffee... 21/25
St Ali Specialty Roasters

DIMATTINA CAFE
173 Clarendon Street, South Melbourne

Refreshing bay breezes waft across South Melbourne and through the large, open windows of Dimattina Cafe on the summery day of our visit. This cafe training venue and batch roaster is designed to soothe, with subdued lighting and a custom-designed wallpaper mural that wraps around two walls and depicts a leafy coffee plantation. Dark timber furnishings complete the colonial ambience.

This beguiling place does breakfast, and boasts an enticing lunch menu of bolognese, risotto, soup, and other hearty dishes best washed down with a good glass of red.

Dimattina sells take-home blends by the bag, and the blend of the week when we visit is a Cuban organic. The polite and friendly barista delivered an espresso that's sharp and acidic, exhibiting bitter chocolate and earthy Brazil nut flavours. It's of medium-to-rich viscosity, and the complex flavours linger long on the palate. Aromas of warm cereal and baked bread enhance the experience. The latte is creamy, robust, and slightly caramel with the addition of half a sugar.

Phone
+613 9929 7444

Trading Hours
mon - fri: 7am - 4pm
sat: 9am - 3pm
sunday closed

Cafe... 21/25
Coffee... 20/25
Dimattina Coffee

MONK BODHI DHARMA
Rear 202 Carlisle Street, Balaclava

Named after a Fifth-Century Buddhist monk from southern India, this modest establishment – hidden behind a dental surgery off Carlisle Street – specialises in coffee and tea, and also serves up hearty vegetarian dishes such as North African ratatouille and date stew. The lads behind the counter are well versed in the coffee-making arts, and will eloquently describe the various in-house brews in the manner of a knowledgeable sommelier.

We try two espressos. The first is from the Zambica Estate, in Zambia, and is extremely tangy and complex with sweet cigar and raw sugar flavours that resolve into an almost lemon-lime zing. It stays long on the palate and feels very clean, with a medium viscosity and no oil. Our second espresso is a Colombian blend that has an earthy taste with hints of nutmeg and a burnt toffee aroma. It lingers on the tongue and eventually becomes slightly sour and ashy. It's richly viscous and clean in the mouth, even after all that complexity. Zen in a cup.

Phone
+613 9534 7250

Trading Hours
mon - fri: 6.30am - 4pm
sat - sun: 8am - 4pm

Cafe... 23/25
Coffee... 24/25
Monk Bodhi Dharma

Inner Melbourne

LITTLE KITCH
113 Puckle Street, Moonee Ponds

Puckle Street is a diverse and lively main drag in the centre of Moonee Ponds, home to cafes, fashion boutiques, a florist and two-dollar shops. Lil Kitch cafe is right in the heart of the action, and one of the busiest of the bunch.

But there is nothing lil when it comes to this cafe — and especially not its menu. The portion sizes can only be described as large, and customers are cramming in for the big burgers with a mountain of fries, oversized focaccia, or big plates of breakfast (served all day). Bet those big dishes keep a small kitchen staff on their toes.

It's coffee o'clock, and I order an espresso. Kitch uses the Giancarlo Arabica blend by Grinders Coffee Co. Named after Giancarlo Giusti – the founder and godfather of Italian coffee in Melbourne – the blend offers a sweet caramel nose, with an earthy flavour and a mild mellowing acidity to finish.

Not the biggest shot around, but again, by no means little.

Phone
+613 9370 0899

Trading Hours
everyday: 7am - 5pm

Cafe... 19/25
Coffee... 16/25
Grinders Coffee

NEW YORK TOMATO
2 New Street, Richmond

First things first. This place is really more on York Street than New Street. Now that we've gotten that off our chest, it is a quiet, tranquil little oasis just a skip from Hoddle Street, all tree-lined and introspective.

Its elusive locale means that it's pretty much the domain of the locals, and despite its discretion and cosy feel, a gentle transition between indoors and outdoors makes the New York Tomato feel larger than it is.

The coffee is an enjoyable brew from Coffee Supreme, and although the espresso is sometimes a little thin, it is a good kick-start to the day. The shot's blueberry entrée mellows to a biscuit flavour with a reasonably short finish. It's not the most characterful cup to be had, but it's a perfectly pleasant complement to the morning papers and a quiet bite in a quiet street.

Phone
+613 9429 0505

Trading Hours
mon - fri: 7.30am - 3.30pm
sat - sun: 8.30am - 3pm

Cafe... 17/25
Coffee... 18/25
Coffee Supreme

ELEVENSES
169 Rankins Road, Kensington

Visiting Elevenses is like dropping in on a friend for coffee. With its vivid yellow walls, single communal table and shelves of condiments and cooking paraphernalia, this homey space feels more like someone's kitchen than a cafe — right down to the idle chit-chat with the barista/cook as he prepares our meals.

While the small menu offers some interesting German-inspired choices, the coffee is the main game. Made from Laos grown beans, and brewed with care on a restored 1964 Boema machine, there are four types to try, with the daily brew dependent on the barista's whim.

We sample the Bruno blend. A rich Italian-style coffee with a distinct caramel aroma, the espresso has a pleasantly tart flavour which coats the tongue and provides just the right level of acidity. The finish is short and sweet, with delicate chocolate undertones. With milk, the chocolate flavours come to the fore, delivering a super-creamy latte I could drink all day. Fortunately, with take-home beans, I can.

Phone
+613 9486 0824

Trading Hours
mon - fri: 7am - 3.30pm
sat - sun: 9am - 3.30pm
wednesday closed

Cafe... 18/25
Coffee... 20/25
Obscura

LITTLE BYRD
160 Union Road, Ascot Vale

In a quiet suburban strip that relies more on convenience than destination shopping, Little Byrd stands out as a beacon of CBD cool. The cosy interior blends modern and vintage touches, along with the left of field — with coloured saucepan-lids stuck on the brick walls.

It's a pram-friendly space, and the wooden furnishings, including a communal table, are sleek and stylish, and a comfy banquette in front of a large window overlooks Union Road. Friendly staff banter with regulars and visitors alike. Breakfast and lunch dishes, most with a Middle Eastern theme, are chalked on a blackboard, but those seeking only a coffee are just as welcome.

My fruity, floral espresso is a pleasure to sip, with a long and sweet aftertaste. The surprisingly light latte is not exactly creamy, but has a fruity, intense flavour. Lucky locals keep this place busy, and it's a destination in its own right.

Phone
+613 9375 1793

Trading Hours
tue - fri: 7.30am - 4.30pm
sat: 8am - 5pm
sun: 9am - 4pm
monday closed

Cafe... 19/25
Coffee... 18/25
Caffe Romeo

Main photograph kindly provided by Brunswick Flour Mill

Inner Melbourne

BRUNSWICK FLOUR MILL
341 Sydney Road, Brunswick

Need a country retreat without the long hours behind the steering wheel? Brunswick Flour Mill is your place.

This inner-city cafe has all the character and ambience of a country bakehouse cafe, and you have to love that smell of freshly baked rustic loaves. (In fact, I'm taken aback when the waitress informs me these dense, chewy loaves are not baked in house but come fresh from The Convent Bakery in Abbotsford.) Display fridges are filled with more tasty treats, like fruit tarts, custard slices and gourmet meat pies.

A steady stream of Brunswick's mix of locals keeps the place grinding, and I file up and order an espresso. Any coffee snobbery is quickly put paid, as the espresso presents a dark golden colour with a nutty aroma and luscious mouthfeel. It's followed by a well-crafted flat white with a silky foam and caramel character.

Life's pretty good in the country.

Phone
+613 9078 0497

Trading Hours
everyday: 7.30am - 5pm

Cafe... 17/25
Coffee... 19/25

The Daily Roast
Rainforest Alliance

BEANS & BAGELS
121 Johnston Street, Fitzroy

The shining silver roaster at the back of the cafe gives an early indication that Beans and Bagels takes its coffee seriously — they hand-roast a variety of single-origin coffees and blends in small batches. As the name suggests, they also take bagels seriously, offering a lengthy selection of super-fresh, New York-inspired bagel sandwiches with names like West Sider (avocado, ham, honey mustard, cream cheese) and Little Italy (salami, semi-dried tomato, salad greens, cream cheese).

The Johnston Street location isn't glamorous, and the cafe itself feels a little like a department store cafeteria (complete with a display cabinet of retail-oriented coffee accessories in the middle of the room, and black vinyl banquette on the periphery).

Happily, the coffee here is superior to your average NYC diner. The espresso is aromatic and chocolaty, with a well-weighted acid kick and bittersweet aftertaste — the perfect extraction for a bright, afternoon flat white.

Phone
+613 9417 0006

Trading Hours
everyday: 8am - 4pm

Cafe... 18/25
Coffee... 19/25
Beans & Bagels

MADE
60 Pin Oak Crescent, Flemington

It's a tight squeeze inside this charming cafe, but the friendly vibe and welcoming attitude from the husband-and-wife owners more than compensates. Just six tables and a tiny serving area, with three tables outside, it's unexpectedly tranquil amid this strip of shops opposite Newmarket station. Even as regulars chat up the owners, the service remains quick and efficient.

There's a small breakfast and lunch menu, with an emphasis on fresh produce and homemade items. Food and coffee are served on gorgeously mismatched vintage china, which fits the overall homey vibe.

The coffee, however, is not 'homey' — it's much better than that. An intense short black is so thick it's almost chewy, and has a long, pleasant aftertaste. My sweet, nutty latte is eminently drinkable with a rich creaminess.

Trading Hours
tue - fri: 7am - 3pm
sat - sun: 8am - 3pm
monday closed

Cafe... 20/25
Coffee... 20/25
Coffee Supreme

Photographs By Tony Mott & Styled By Claire Larrit Evans. Kindly provided by Market Lane Coffee

MARKET LANE COFFEE
Shop 13, Prahran Market, South Yarra

Tucked away in a corner of the Prahran Market, this cafe and micro-roaster approaches its work with passion and knowledge. Staff will gladly explain the difference between espresso and filter (or pour-over) methods of brewing, and a blackboard diagram offers tasting notes.

We try a filter coffee made from Red Bourbon beans from El Salvador; it's fruity and refreshing to taste, and very smooth and subtle with a short, clean finish. This is the cafe's preferred brewing method as it's gentle on the bean and retains nuanced flavours. The espresso uses the seasonal blend (currently a Brazilian and Kenyan mix) and exhibits citrus flavours which eventually resolve into toasted fruit-bread and cinnamon. It's lightly oily with a rich, velvet viscosity and caramel-toffee aroma.

Market Lane Coffee also sells its single-estate and other coffees by the bag. And those overburdened by shopping jeeps or prams needn't worry — this spacious establishment seems specially designed for encumbered shoppers.

Phone
+613 9804 7434

Trading Hours
tue - sat: 7am - 5pm
sun: 9am - 3pm
monday closed

Cafe... 23/25
Coffee... 23/25
Market Lane Coffee

Inner Melbourne

TOBY'S ESTATE
29 Weston Street, Brunswick

In his first Melbourne store, Sydneysider Toby Smith shares his passion for all things caffeinated. This rustic converted warehouse is a shrine to the bean, offering a range of fair trade single origin coffees (plus a selection of teas and drinking chocolates), as well as a school for budding baristas.

It's also a great place for a lazy Sunday brunch. The small menu is packed with breakfast favourites, along with a range of toasties for the Breville-addicted. Late risers, however, take note: the kitchen closes at 2:30pm, although cakes and cookies are available if you're sweet-toothed or desperate.

We sample the Sumatra Gayo Mountain. With its strong herbal aroma and mouth-tingling acidity, the espresso is a tangy drop with a rich mouthfeel that ends in a surprisingly rounded finish. The latte – perfectly executed by master roaster and barista Chris – is a work of art. A delicate fern floats atop a thick foam that gives way to a velvety smooth brew, still big on flavour. Great stuff, for a Sydneysider.

Phone
+613 9009 5462

Trading Hours
tue - sun: 9am - 4pm
monday closed

Cafe... 22/25
Coffee... 20/25
Toby's Estate

NORTH
717 Rathdowne Street, Carlton North

North of the CBD, amid the laid-back seclusion of Rathdowne's leafy village enclave, terrace shops nestle beneath collective verandas, and it's only the glossy malachite tiles that distinguish North from its neighbours. You can unwind outside where spores waft down from trees, attempting a new life in your lap or your latte. Or you can escape indoors for less nature and more menu.

Beneath its lackadaisical crema, glazed colours flash on my short black. Tasting strongly sour and bitter, it lacks a touch of sweetness to fill out its flavour. In pleasing contrast, the latte is sweet and animated, impressive with its feathery adornment and rich as a classic cream sauce.

Before you exit, look to the wall on the side of the door, where a suited cat fares you well with a tip of his hat. Assure him you'll be back for more from the lip-licking menu.

Phone
+613 9348 1276

Trading Hours
mon - fri: 8am - 4pm
sat - sun: 8.30am - 5pm

Cafe... 20/25
Coffee... 16/25
Coffee Supreme

COLLECTIVE ESPRESSO
3 Cookson Street, Camberwell

As the name suggests, Collective Espresso is all about sociable caffeination, and if that's your bag then this is the place to pack it. The cafe may be small in size, but an extension is under way as we go to print, and this simple yet chic place is assuredly set to grow in stature.

Neutral colours dominate, and the menu is a standard blackboard — albeit with some lovely options. A long communal table unfurls in the centre of the cafe, urging that trademark socialisation in the communal drinking space.

I'm torn between a fresh Danish pastry or savoury baguette, and the coffee arrives as a fortunate distraction. The espresso is herby in aroma and surprisingly sharp; the flavour is a little bitter, and the aftertaste surprisingly short and mild. My cappuccino is chocolaty and vibrant, with an enveloping sweetness and velvety mouthfeel — the smoothest conversation-starter imaginable.

Phone
+613 9882 8995

Trading Hours
mon - fri: 7am - 5pm
sat - sun: 8am - 4pm

Cafe... 18/25
Coffee... 19/25
5 Senses Coffee

PORGIE + MR JONES
291 Auburn Road, Hawthorn

This airy, light-filled cafe – a former violineri workshop – enjoys rustic décor and an immediate homey feel. But there's a certain, urban cool in quirky touches like a red chair suspended in the corner of the ceiling, terracotta herb pots perched on a wall, and low-flying pendant lights which brood over a long timber table.

A busy Saturday morning has the two main rooms and rear outdoor courtyard near-full of locals: young families, middle-aged intellectual types and arty students. There's a low riot of indie music battling it out against the spurting, whirling and clang of the coffee machine.

My espresso arrives quickly, breezing with soft herbaceous and floral scents. The flavour is surprisingly complex: rich spices give way to black berries and a chocolate finish, and it's like silk on the palate. A spirited acidity ensures the coffee lingers in the mouth. In all, an eclectic shop with a consistently good drop.

Phone
+613 9882 2955

Trading Hours
mon - fri: 8am - 4pm
sat - sun: 8.30am - 4pm

Cafe... 21/25
Coffee... 21/25
Allpress Espresso

BUTTERFLY CAFE
25 Cookson Street, Camberwell

Butterfly Cafe is something of a retro time-warp: red and orange in décor, with white leafy wallpaper on one wall and striped cushioned booths for seating. The loud colours certainly make the most of the tiny space — as do the casual and friendly staff.

The food, however, is decidedly modern in its global scope, with a good mix of pides, baguettes, salads and jaffles to select from. The Nutella and Banana Jaffle looks a favourite with the local crowd, despite the temptations of muffins, cakes and slices in the front cabinet.

As for the coffee, my espresso has a pleasant nutty aroma, with a salty flavour that's rich in body but still perfectly elegant in terms of acidity. My cappuccino proves less creamy on the palate and – unfortunately – a little more watery. Its acidity is milder, but the aftertaste is a lot sweeter and longer, and the aroma more caramelly.

Trading Hours
mon - fri: 7.30am - 4pm
sat: 8am - 4pm
sunday closed

Cafe... 15/25
Coffee... 14/25
Butterfly Blend

MINIMO
822 Sydney Road, Brunswick

Inner Melbourne

As Sydney Road approaches the Coburg border, the cut of pedestrians' jeans becomes noticeably looser, edgy boutiques give way to not-so-edgy crash repairers, and cafes swap hipster street-smarts for easy, affable charm. Case in point, Minimo, where you're likely to be welcomed with a sample of freshly baked caramel slice.

The space itself isn't groundbreaking, but it is pleasant: polished concrete floors are complemented by a neutral palette and dark timber furniture; natural light streams in through floor-to-ceiling glass, illuminating a communal table strewn with weekend papers. It's the kind of place where you can make yourself at home, with a tray of sweetly haemorrhaging pain au chocolat straight from the oven, or the trademark spicy Moroccan beef pie floater.

The friendly folk do justice to fine beans from Atomica, extracting full-bodied, pitch-black espresso topped with a dense tan crema. The shot boasts aromatic vanilla notes and a persistent nutty flavour that lingers long after the last drop.

Phone
+613 9383 2083

Trading Hours
mon: 7.30am - 4.30pm
wed - fri: 7.30am - 4.30pm
sat - sun: 9am - 4pm
tuesday closed

Cafe... 19/25
Coffee... 19/25
Atomica

RAY CAFE
332 Victoria Street, Brunswick

Brunswick is cool, in the way that people who are cool don't need to tell you that they're cool. Brunswick never told anyone it was cool. The embodiment of this savoir faire is Ray Cafe, on Victoria Street. If you're looking for an escape from the hubbub of Sydney Road, you won't find it here. At peak times, this place has a frenetic pulse that bursts with the energy of the recently installed art crowd.

The food is a fantastic conglomerate of Mediterranean, Middle Eastern and Asian influences, well-priced and generously proportioned. The décor is requisitely uncomplicated and is favoured by the locals, most of whom are on a first-name basis with the waitstaff.

The barista works the coffee machine like a shovel-man at the boiler of a steam engine. Thankfully, the quality doesn't suffer for the formidable output, and the espresso extraction is a creamy brew from Atomica beans, rich and nutty with a long tobacco finish.

Phone
+613 9380 8593

Trading Hours
mon - fri: 7.30am - 5pm
sat - sun: 8am - 5pm

Cafe... 18/25
Coffee... 17/25
Atomica

JULIO
171 Miller Street, Fitzroy North

North Fitzroy locals love Julio, and visitors from elsewhere wish they were North Fitzroy locals so they could love Julio more regularly. On a quiet street opposite a primary school in a residential pocket, this simple cafe is your fantasy corner-store.

Blond timber joinery, neat little tables and chairs, a brick floor and tall communal table establish a warm aesthetic. It's kid-friendly – there's a well-stocked toy box and the staff aren't fussed by stepping over sprawling toddlers – without being a 'kiddie cafe'. And you walk through the vegetable store on your way to the bathroom. It feels like you've just dropped in on an old friend. A friend who makes glorious jam doughnuts, and sardine, lemon and harissa toasted sandwiches.

Happily, Julio does a star turn as a barista too, extracting a syrupy espresso with a super-dense golden crema, fruity aroma, a delicate dusting of cocoa on the tongue and plenty of fresh acidity.

Phone
+613 9489 7814

Trading Hours
everyday: 7.30am - 4pm

Cafe... 19/25
Coffee... 19/25
Coffee Supreme

Main Photograph kindly provided by Brunswick East Project

BRUNSWICK EAST PROJECT
438 Lygon Street, Brunswick East

The words 'hand crafted' are subtly frosted onto the Project's window, and they set the tone for the cafe. Care and heart are apparent in the ceramics that stand in for coffee cups — an homage, perhaps, to Brunswick's pottery-making past.

Photography, paintings and sculptures by locals feature about the cafe, along with less local, drought-resistant greenery and sacks of bean-bulging hessian.

There's an obligatory bicycle chained up outside, and room about the roaster to discuss yoga poses, parenting, academic theses or a perfect home-brewed espresso.

The Padre blend, in espresso form, is as thin as a slip, with a rich toffee nose and provocative acidity — worth missing the tram for. The malt aroma of my latte gives way to a brittle burst of brandy-snap on the palate.

Phone
+613 9939 8422

Trading Hours
tue - sun: 8am - 4pm
monday closed

Cafe... 22/25
Coffee... 21/25
Padre Coffee

Inner Melbourne

SEVEN A.M.
155 Bay Street, Port Melbourne

If the very notion of 7am fills you with foreboding, Seven A.M. – the cafe – is a zippy little shop-front establishment in Port Melbourne that will help you through to 8am with a serve or two of Coffee Supreme's Boxer Blend.

Sitting at the cafe's communal table, we enjoy an espresso that's oily on the tongue with dark chocolate and berry flavours. It feels good in the mouth, boasting a long finish and bittersweet butternut-snap aftertaste. The affogato is a refreshing choice on a warm day.

Seven:am does breakfast and lunch, with the option of the 'boardroom' — a long table upstairs which can be booked for meetings and celebrations. There are also plans to open for dinner. The décor and music is just right for those of us who need to be eased into the day: the smooth tunes are unobtrusive, and the no-fuss fit-out features exposed brick walls decked with gig posters and travel photos — now that you're awake.

Phone
+613 9078 5776

Trading Hours
mon - sat: 7am - 3pm
sun: 8am - 3pm

Cafe... 19/25
Coffee... 19/25
Coffee Supreme

HOME BARISTA INSTITUTE
225 Victoria Street, West Melbourne

Caffeine addicts need look no further for their hit — everything coffee-related is here. The experience starts with the intoxicating coffee aroma that lingers in the doorway. Inside, coffee is everywhere: instruction videos play on the TV above the machine; photos of barista course participants are stuck under the laminated table tops; and flip-folders on each table contain tips and trivia.

Breakfast and lunch are available, but the focus is on coffee. Not surprisingly, the coffees are textbook perfect: the short black has a caramel crema and an intense, strong body. The complex mix of berries, wood and chocolate is delicious, with a long aftertaste. A practised rosetta adorns the golden-brown latte, which is smooth, creamy, rich — and finished all too quickly.

The only downside is that this place no longer opens on weekends, so Queen Victoria Market shoppers can only get their fix during the week.

Phone
+613 9328 1090

Trading Hours
mon - fri: 7am - 2pm
saturday & sunday closed

Cafe... 20/25
Coffee... 22/25
Home Barista Institute Blend

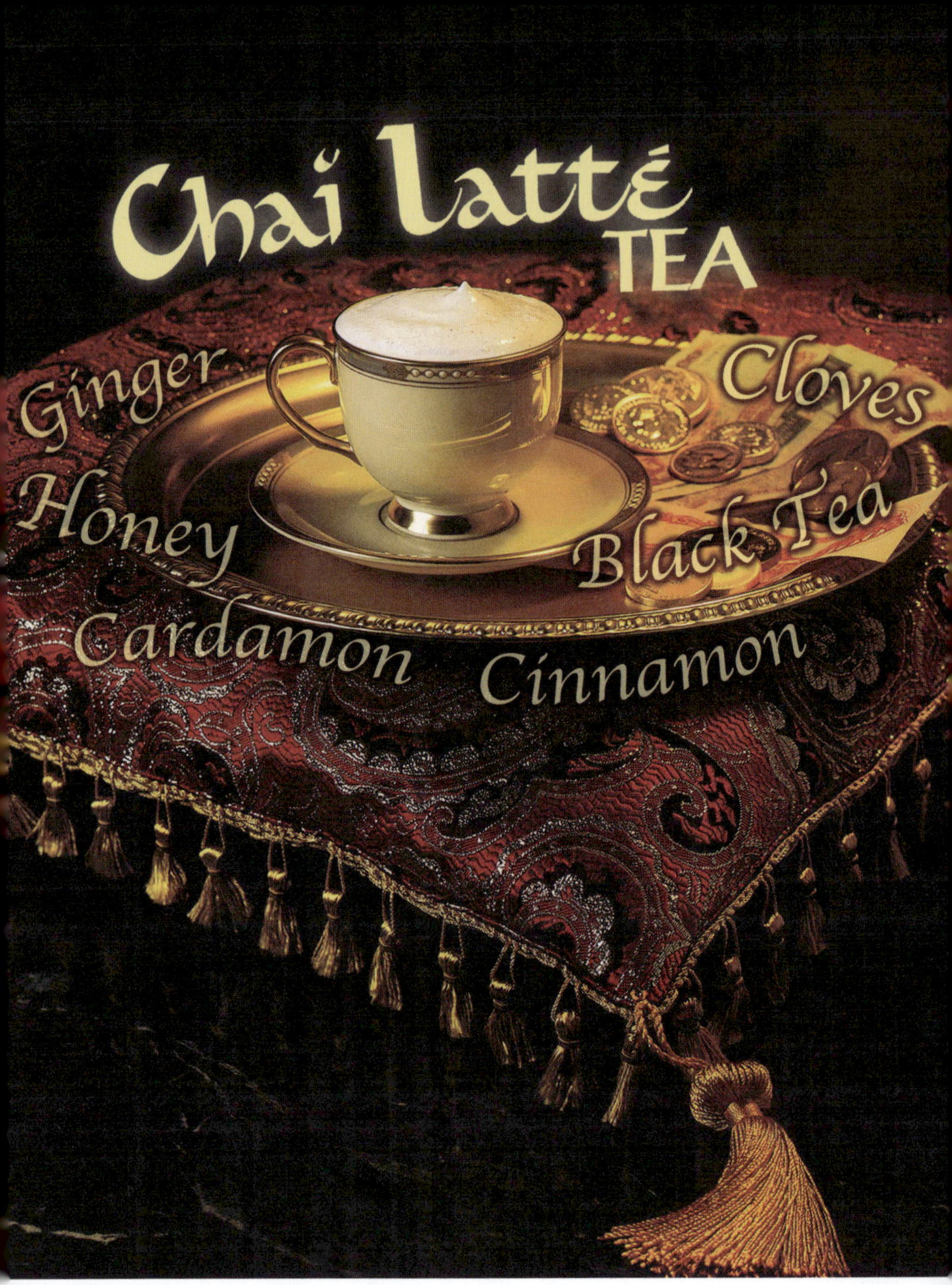
Chai latté
TEA
Ginger
Cloves
Honey
Black Tea
Cardamon
Cinnamon

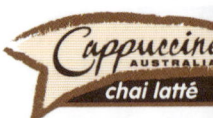

The Tea Room
National Gallery of Victoria
Level 1, NGV, 180 St Kilda Road, Melbourne

"It's the most subtly perfumed white tea I've encountered — a floral evolution in the pot."

There's a moment as you step into the moody surrounds of the NGV Tea Room, where the usual silence of the gallery deepens just a little bit further. Settling in for afternoon tea, it's a moment of sheer serenity ~ heightened by the play of light cast by the gallery's famous water wall. The Tea Room has an open café-style setting, yet achieves an intimacy from its corner spot peering out at the rest of the gallery. Bucket seats are reflected in gilt-edged mirrors, but it's the counter display of multicoloured cakes and confections that catches the eye.

Trading Hours
10am - 4.30pm
Closed Tuesday.

Contact
(03) 8620 2431
www.ngv.vic.gov.au

A smiling waitress in teapot motif skirt presents us with the drinks menu; there's coffee on offer, but with a comprehensive range of teas selected by Larsen Thompson Teas, this really is all about the leaf. So we order the afternoon tea to share and choose the Jin Mao Hou ~ Golden Monkey black tea ~ to go with it. Then, in our excitement, we order an additional pot of Bai Hao Yin Zhen ~ Silver Needle white tea ~ with its promise of a 'sweet floral finish'.

An impressive three-tiered cake stand spills over with the requisite pastries, scones and macaroons. The Golden Monkey (named for it's resemblance to monkey claws) arrives in an ornate teapot, and dances brightly in the mouth before settling into a slightly smoky finish after some extra brewing. It's a first flush, early spring tea and one of the Tea Room's most popular black brews.

However, it's the Silver Needle that steals our hearts. Delivered in a shorter and more modern teapot, this velvety tea blossoms into a delicate Jasmine finish that only improves with brewing. It's the most subtly perfumed white tea I've encountered ~ a floral evolution in the pot.

What better place to experience the art of afternoon tea?

Red Monkey Tea House

470 Victoria Street, North Melbourne

"The tea arrives with a heady aroma, overflowing with exotic star anise and peppery tones."

It's early on a Saturday night when we stop by the Red Monkey Tea House, and despite being the first customers (like early, awkward guests at a dinner party) we're instantly welcomed. Hidden from the street behind unassuming blinds, it's all red-lit Korean kung-fu flare and monkey motifs within.

A modest bar presides over the relaxed front room, with an eski serving as countertop icebox. Ain't nothing fancy here, just congenial chitchat and a corridor to the intimate suburban beer garden.

Trading Hours
Tues - Thurs 4pm - 11pm
Fri & Sat 4pm - 1am
Sun 4pm - 11pm

Contact
(03) 9326 7572
www.redmonkeyteahouse.com

When we ask to see the tea menu, we're told they've been ripped by "tatty edges" ~ testament to Red Monkey's popularity. Replacements are in order, but in the meantime the barman is happy to make suggestions based on what kind of flavour profiles we like, or to go through each of the roughly 60 teas for us. Now that's dedication to the leaf.

We sidestep the tea-infused cocktails (think jasmine tea gin) for a chai martini, and then trawl through an array of promising little tea boxes filled with everything from Golden Monkey to Eastern Sunrise, settling eventually on a pot of White Spice.

The tea arrives with a heady aroma, overflowing with exotic star anise and peppery tones. And then the martini knocks our socks off. Freshly brewed chai kicks out cassia, cloves and liquorice, delivered with toffee tones of sugar syrup and all mixed up with vodka and a cinnamon stick. It's potent, earthy and full of spice.

There's tapas-style food as well, but it's the drinks that provide the monkey magic.

Oriental Tea House
455 Chapel Street, South Yarra, Melbourne

"We're already awash with flavour, and the Dim Sum hasn't even arrived."

The red-pillared surrounds of the Oriental Tea House almost feels like downtown Hong-Kong ~ were it not for Chapel Street outside. An East-meets-West vibe hangs in the air, with reproduction 1940s Shanghai-darling posters and lanterns dangling from above. The front room is filled with shelves of brightly coloured tea-boxes which contain all manner of leaves: white and black, fruit infusions and medicinal roots. The Tea House is part of a small chain (with sister stores in Chadstone and the CBD), but it's lost none of its charm through expansion.

Trading Hours
Everyday from 10am till late.
……………………………………

Contact
(03) 9826 0168
www.orientalteahouse.com.au

Further in, cabinets display various tea trinkets, and tasting stations offer thimbleful taste-tests of obscure brews. Drawers filled with Chinese medicines cover an entire wall, and you can book a consultation. But plenty of people simply stop by for a Yum Cha feed with their chai.

We're ushered to a table for two on a raised platform, and order Dim Sum ~ because who can resist a medley of dumplings to complement a delicate cup? The tea menu is long and wanders effortlessly from traditional to iced teas, and even tea cocktails. Despite the appeal of a Russian Spy in Shanghai (gunpowder tea and vodka), we teetotal and order an Enhance BeauTEA (rose) and an Antioxidant SpecialTEA (jasmine and lychee).

Both arrive in large yet delicate glass mugs with lids to trap the fragile aromas. The Enhance mug cradles a handful of tightly curled pale-pink rosebuds, gently bobbing away; it delivers a bright, clean and grassy mouthful, best described as pretty ~ in the cup and the mouth.

And the Antioxidant is just as beautiful, arriving as a ball of leaves before unfurling in an explosion of pointy green tendrils ~ and then a fruity freshness in the mouth. We're already awash with flavour, and the Dim Sum hasn't even arrived.

Photos provided by Oriental Tea House.

Traditional Afternoon Tea at Hotel Windsor

111 Spring Street, Melbourne

"the tea is all but forgotten when the celebrated three-tiered cake plate arrives"

Tea at the Windsor is an occasion ~ with all the attendant planning and anticipation. It starts with detailed descriptions when you call to make a reservation (designed to have you salivating before you've even secured a table). Happily, once you've frocked up and worked yourself into a giddy frenzy, the experience lives up to the expectation.

The maître d' greets us at the door and hands us gently over to our waiter, who is ceremoniously charged with our care. Afternoon tea here is a two-hour affair; but before we can wonder who could possibly need two hours for tea, we pause in the refined surrounds and realise ~ we do. Seated at our beautifully appointed table with a glass of sparkling rosé, every pain has been taken to put us at our ease.

Trading Hours
Reservations Essential.
Mon - Fri   2.30pm - 4.30pm
Sat & Sun 12pm - 2pm &
                  2.30pm - 4.30pm

Contact
(03) 9633 6004
www.thehotelwindsor.com.au

There are herbal infusions and coffee on offer, but afternoon tea without the tea seems to miss the point, so we order a pot of the Windsor's special House blend. Lightly smoky with a beautiful grassy fragrance and a warm amber glow in the cup, it benefits from a little extra brewing time, developing fuller flavours and a complex finish.

However, the tea is all but forgotten when the celebrated three-tiered cake plate arrives. On top are fresh scones, still warm. Beneath them is everything from perfectly formed French macaroons to miniature mango and chocolate tarts, all fashioned, painstakingly, in-house.

Two hours later, with a top up of hot water to our pot, we've only just gotten through the tiers (albeit at an entirely leisurely pace). It's been an almost historic event ~ a refined, hat-and-gloves occasion which the Windsor has been perfecting since 1883. Although we suspect they attained perfection a while back.

Photos provided by Hotel Windsor.

The Beginner's Guide to Tea

By Selina Altomonte

We've come a long way since Lan-choo, baby. And while there's nothing wrong with jiggling the old tea bag with milk and sugar for your morning cuppa, there's so much more to be found in a cup.

Across the world, tea is the most consumed beverage after water, but it's no exaggeration to say most tea drinkers ~ or at least, novice tea drinkers ~ have got it all wrong. "The most common mistakes made would have to be brewing a tea for too long, or burning your tea," says Jenni Longden, Tea Trainer at leading tea emporium T2.

"The tea leaf contains tannin which, when left to brew too long can completely ruin the tea by making it taste bitter, astringent and unpleasant," she explains. So that cup or pot of tea you've forgotten about while chatting or distracted by work is good as gone if neglected for more than five minutes — and that's if you're making a resilient black brew. Pour it on the garden and start again if you want to get any enjoyment out of drinking it.

The second biggest problem is burning your tea, as different teas need to be brewed at different temperatures. A strong English Breakfast, for example, needs water just off the boil to bring out its kick, but, as Jenni points out, "When brewing delicate teas like green tea (or the rare white and yellow teas), boiling water burns the leaf and intensifies the bitter taste of tannin. Avoid this by using off the boil water: we suggest around 80°C for most green, yellow and white teas." If you've dabbled in green teas or senchas in the past and found them too bitter, chances are you've scorched the leaves. Give it another go at the right temperature and you might have a tea revelation.

Image supplied by The Oriental Tea House.

Usually, you can find a suggested steeping time on your tea's packaging, but follow this general guide (noting that longer is stronger):

Black Tea
95ºC; 2-5 minutes

Earl Grey
95ºC; 3-5 minutes

Oolong
90ºC; 2-4 minutes

White Tea
85ºC; 3-5 minutes

Green Tea
80ºC; 1-3 minutes

Jasmine
80ºC; 5-10 minutes

Peppermint
90ºC; 2-4 minutes

Rooibos
100ºC; 4-6 minutes

Chai
100ºC; 5-10 minutes
(can also be brewed in a saucepan over low heat)

Herbal Infusions/Tisanes
95ºC; 3-5 minutes

Tea *vs* Tisane

All tea is made from the leaves of the same plant: Camellia sinensis. The differences lie in what happens to the leaves after they've been picked. Black teas have been fermented, green tea is unfermented while oolong is semi-fermented. White tea, prized for its delicate flavour, is made from the first buds picked after winter and fermented for the shortest amount of time.

An infusion or tisane is made using flowers (such as chamomile), roots (dandelion), herbs and leaves of other plants (peppermint).

Image supplied by The Oriental Tea House.

Kit to drink

Half the joy of tea drinking is all the little accoutrements you'll need.

Jenni suggests the following:

* A good teapot with a clean and steady pour and inbuilt infuser.
* A favourite teacup (typically with a finer lip than a coffee cup).
* Airtight storage in glass or tin.
* A proper measuring teaspoon for the tea leaves.
* A thermometer for the more delicate teas.

To brew the perfect pot, start with fresh and preferably filtered cold water. (Never re-boil water for tea as it will contain little oxygen and result in a flat flavour.) Pour a little of the boiled water into your teapot and swirl it around ~ a warmed teapot keeps the water at the optimum temperature for the tea. Add a teaspoon of tea for each person plus 'one for the pot', then pour over the boiled water. Steep for the required time for your tea. The Chinese call the unfurling of the leaves 'the dance of agony', and if you're a bit of a voyeur, invest in a glass teapot.

Taking it to
the next level

Tea bags may be the most convenient option, but the first step in your tea education is to graduate to loose leaf. A good-quality, fresh-leaf tea is ideal, says tea master Tjok Gde Kerthyasa, who was responsible for revitalising the high tea service at The Observatory Hotel in Sydney and has teamed with Arthur Tong to create Tea Craft, offering fine teas and tearwares. Loose leaf produces more flavour, as essential oils are captured if the leaves are in direct contact with the water. "There are many teas on the market these days, some exotic, others utilitarian," says Tjok. "It's always a good move to contact a specialist tea purveyor to talk about your preferences."

Tea tasting can be as intricate and complex as for wine or coffee, and with a little mindfulness, it's easy to gain a deeper enjoyment for something you drink every day. If you want to develop your tea appreciation skills, Tjok suggests you start by trying a good single estate Assam tea and comparing it to your regular cup. Or look for exotic teas you've never tried before, and explore different ways of serving tea, such as traditional Chinese methods.

When it comes to training your tastebuds, Jenni says there are three things you should focus on: appearance, smell, and taste.

"For a good-quality black, and white tea, the liquid should appear clear (without cloudiness); green teas can be a little cloudy," she explains. *"The colour usually indicates how heavy the taste will be: the darker the brew, the more robust the taste. Finally, a good tea should always smell sweet and fresh. If your nose picks up a hay aroma, musty, oily smell or another taint, this is an indication of a poor-quality tea."*

Enjoy each cup

For Verity Fisher, who plays with different blends for her range, Joie de Tea, and blogs about her taste for the leaf at joiedetea.blogspot.com, tea drinking is much more than a pastime. "I love its variety of colours, flavours and shapes, and the incredible care that goes into its manufacture," she says. "I love its comfort value; its energising yet simultaneously relaxing qualities.'

Beyond flavour, the ritual of tea drinking can become an essential part of your morning pick-me-up, mid-arvo recharge or evening wind-down. Make it as simple as you want, like busting out your brightest Pantone mug, or as special as dusting off Nanna's favourite pot. "I have a few rituals," says Verity, "but I try to take time to enjoy the tea visually, the way it smells and so on."

For Tjok, tea drinking is also enhanced by its visual elements. "To enjoy tea it is important to drink it from a nice cup – fine bone china or fine porcelain are my personal favourites, in plain white so I can see the colour of the tea."

And don't be afraid to experiment. Follow Verity's lead and play with different teas to create your own blends, or if you want more kick to your cup, add more leaves (but don't increase the steeping time to match). Most importantly, says Jenni, "Take time out. Tea has a history of being the 'restful' drink. Why not shut out the world for a while and enjoy?"

simply a beautiful way to relax and kick back

Tea Drop's
Oolong Rose

there's tea and then there's the whole leaf experience

High Tea at The Observatory Hotel

89-113 Kent Street, Sydney

"the most luxurious collection of teas in Australia."

Trading Hours
By appointment only.
Mon - Fri   2.30pm - 5pm
Sat & Sun 2pm - 4.30pm

....

Contact
(02) 9256 2215
www.observatoryhotel.com.au

It's hard to believe the Observatory Hotel's Globe Bar has only been around since the early '90s (and no, that's not the 1890s). Resplendent in old world glamour, it comes complete with grandfather clock, antique globe (hence the name), and framed illustrations that look as if they've been torn from early editions of the New Yorker.

Early into the tea service, it seems patrons feel the need to speak in hushed tones as if we actually are in the drawing room of some ancient mansion, but it isn't long before the Champagne some are enjoying in lieu of tea takes effect, and excited chitchat and laughter bursts around the room.

But as tempting as a glass of bubbly can be at 2pm on a Sunday afternoon, the tea here shouldn't be missed. The menu of 19 speciality teas, ranging from Organic Gunpowder Green to stimulating Warm Spice, has been hand-picked by tea master Tjok Gde Kerthyasa, who describes this selection as "the most luxurious collection of teas in Australia".

It's blistering hot outside, so I need something light and refreshing. The Harbour Breeze sounds like it will hit the spot, and it arrives in a beautifully patterned antique teapot ~ each of us at the table is treated to a different one, apparently also hand-picked from around the world. Harbour Breeze lives up to its name, with uplifting lemongrass and mint. I can't quite make out the other flavours, but our affable waitress tells me the blend includes fennel and elderberries. Even when allowed to cool (while scoffing smoked salmon, honey and caper sandwiches and tiny opera cakes topped with gold leaf), the flavours stay distinct and refreshing.

As I sit back to enjoy the last of the mini crème brûlées, I spot tea-leaf reader extraordinaire Lyndel Barker-Revell flitting around the tables, peering into the fine china cups to reveal what the leaves have to say. Exotic blends, Champagne, silver service and divination after you've taken your last sip and enjoyed every crumb ~ afternoon tea doesn't get any more indulgent than this.

THE KETTLE THAT MAKES TEA
With auto lower and lift basket

The secret to drawing out the best aroma and flavour from tea is to brew it right.

According to leading tea experts, there are two common mistakes made when brewing tea: using water at the wrong temperature and brewing for the incorrect amount of time. To master the art of tea, it's essential to understand the optimum conditions for each variety.

So how do you know how long and hot to brew tea?

The Breville Automatic Tea Maker and Kettle is a great advantage to even the most experienced tea connoisseur. Sleek and smart, it boils water at the right temperature for your favourite tea, infuses it for the correct time and keeps it warm – so you can enjoy that second cup even sooner.

For further information, visit **www.breville.com.au**

Breville

The Victoria Room
Level 1, 235 Victoria Street, Darlinghurst, Sydney

"I try on their Earl Grey Premium... and it's a bold brew, scented with natural bergamot oil."

Push through the heavy wooden doors and let your eyes adjust to the candlelit stairway leading up to The Victoria Room. Jewel-hued wallpapers, Chesterfield sofas and hunting-themed art complete the British-Raj chic.

Weekends here are dedicated to the ritual of high tea, and the space, unsurprisingly, is dominated by women dolled up for drinks served with gossip (today, there's even a head-turning duo dressed to the nines with finger curls, pussy-bow blouses and coquettish cat's-eye glasses).

Trading Hours
Sat   12pm - 5pm
Sun   1pm - 5pm
Bookings highly recommended.
....

Contact
(02) 9357 4488
www.thevictoriaroom.com

The maître d' leads me to a small table enveloped by the low crimson glow of an antique lamp, where I sink into a throne-like chair. The tea menu includes herbal and fruit infusions, along with classics such as English Breakfast Supreme and Russian Caravan ~ all made from GM-free leaves. I try on their Earl Grey Premium (my usual poison), and it's a bold brew, scented with natural bergamot oil. It's a lovely fusion of florals and citrus rind, but gets bitter with top-ups, so isn't one to linger over. (That would be the brooding Scottish Breakfast.)

The food platter, however, *is* one to take your time with. The sandwiches, including the old-school shaved cucumber, crème fraîche and dill, are entirely moreish; the fluffy scones with organic strawberry jam and chantilly cream are divine. Miniature sweets include a chocolate mousse that's had just enough of a whipping to hold up a fresh raspberry, and a red velvet cupcake straight from the Mad Hatter's table.

The room, as usual, is full, but the service is still attentive, and at the end of our session we're asked if there's anything we'd like to bring home ~ the teas are available in a luxury hamper so you can make the experience last. If only you could take the Victoria Room's moody decadence out the door too.

Photos provided by The Victoria Room

The Tea Centre Sydney

The Glasshouse, 146 Pitt Street Mall, Sydney

"Organic Assam Tea ~ tannic, robust and punchy, it does the job."

The Saturday afternoon is dwindling, which could explain why this pocket of the Glasshouse in Pitt Street Mall is so oddly quiet. But this makes the Tea Centre all the easier to find: it's the only place people are heading to.

This tiny tea room is one of eight branches across Australia, but despite the simple set-up (leather banquette, café-standard tables), this is no cookie-cutter institution. For one thing, the world's biggest China teapot is apparently in the window, along with colourful loose leaf displays.

Trading Hours
Mon - Fri   9am - 5.30pm
Thurs   9am - 8pm
Sat   10am - 5pm

Contact
(02) 9223 9909
www.theteacentre.com.au

There are also shelves of exotic paraphernalia and marvellous canisters, pretty teacups and teapots to buy. And taking pride of place behind the counter, a floor-to-ceiling collection of giant tins containing house blends ~ each available to try in the café or buy for home.

I take a seat by the window and flip through the four-page tea menu: all preservative and artificial-flavour free, flown into Australia every 4-6 weeks for freshness, and brewed with filtered water. My partner would usually be settling in for a double macchiato, so asks our waiter for an "afternoon hit" tea. He suggests an Organic Assam ~ tannic, robust and punchy, it does the job.

I try out a herbal infusion dubbed 'Bright Eyed and Bushy Tailed'. A blend of liquorice, Siberian ginseng, damiana, gotu kola, peppermint, spearmint and rose petals, it arrives in a fire-engine-red Zero teapot.

My first cup has a distinct smoky flavour, but after the tea mellows in the pot it develops a sweeter complexity: the unmistakable earthy flavour of ginseng and a viscous smack of honey. It's an evolution in a tea cup, and I leave still trying to pick apart the flavours, bright eyed and fired up about how good tea can be.

Taka Tea Garden
320 New South Head Road, Double Bay, Sydney

"...a quiet, cosy space, cocooned by pristine rows of clay teapots, handmade ceramics and tea accoutrements."

Double Bay certainly has changed since its heady days as Sydney's epicentre of glitz. Sure, there are still some uber-boutiques clinging on, but today's Doublay-vay has a couple of great quirks to make it worth the visit, one being the little house of Zen on New South Head Road: Taka Tea Garden.

It's a quiet, cosy space, cocooned by pristine rows of clay teapots, handmade ceramics and tea accoutrements.

Trading Hours
Tues - Sat 1pm -6pm
....

Contact
(02) 9362 1777
www.takateagarden.com.au

Pick up some premium green teas from Japan, Taiwan and China, but stay to enjoy the highly prized gyokuro – the highest grade of Japanese green tea. It's made from the youngest, freshest leaves of tea trees shaded from direct sunlight for 20 days before harvest ~ this contributes to the tea's brilliant colour, smooth flavour and high levels of antioxidants.

Owner Taka Pan himself brews the gyokuro, keeping the mood light as he chuckles and listens to jazz as he goes about his work. It arrives in a little glass orb of a teapot, so I can enjoy its vivid apple-green hue, along with a couple of surprises: a serve of roasted peas and sweet red bean paste. I'm starting to wonder if I needed to order that slice of green tea cake too. The tea, brewed at 60°C, is ready to drink immediately ~ its aroma is almost seaweed-like, and the first cup stimulates the back and sides of the tongue with a faint bitterness, but it's entirely pleasant, fresh and clean. The second cup brings out its sweetness and grassiness.

I peer into the pot and notice the leaves look fresh ~ as though just picked. Taka notices my interest and brings over some soy sauce and a tiny bowl. Apparently, gyokuro's unfermented leaves can be eaten after brewing ~ this way, you can enjoy its health benefits to the full. It's like eating steamed Asian greens ~ subtle but flavoursome. Somehow, my cup of tea has turned into a full-blown meal, and I leave heavier than intended, but a little more enlightened.

two leaves and a bud
TEA COMPANY

Whole Leaf Organic Tea Sachets

At two leaves and a bud we only use the finest teas, grown in a single geographic region using traditional growing methods. We travel the world to bring you...

- Black Teas
- Green Teas
- Chai Teas
- Red Teas
- White Teas
- Herbal Teas

...a better cuppa' tea

info@cappuccine.com.au
cappuccine.com.au
P.O. Box 7019
Alexandria NSW 2015

Tel: 1300 788 355
Fax: 02 8338 8540

www.cappuccine.com.au

a new dimension to an old classic

English Breakfast

Ceylon Strong

Supreme Earl Grey

Lavender Grey

Malabar Chai

Spring Green

Honeydew Green

Oolong Rose

Cleopatra's Champagne

Peppermint

Moroccan Mint

Fruits of Eden

Lemongrass Ginger

the whole leaf experience
www.teadrop.com

14/51 Moreland Road, East Coburg, VIC 3058, Australia
Australia Ph: 1300 832 376 • International Ph:+61393832300
enquiries@teadrop.com.au

Selina Altomonte

TEA LOVE
in the age of coffee

Tell me whether you're a coffee or tea drinker, and I'll tell you what kind of person you are. Well, not so long ago, at least, you could make some un-PC assumptions about those who fell in the coffee-drinking camp: fast-living, cosmopolitan, sweaty-palmed if they haven't had their 3pm hit. Meanwhile, tea drinkers would have their knitting needles in one hand and their Queen Elizabeth coronation mug in the other.

We may have all become a little more enlightened, or simply dazzled by the colourful window displays of T2's expanding empire, but tea is enjoying a full-blown revival. And coffee drinkers are along for the ride, introducing a daily green tea for an antioxidant boost, or alternating espressos with a good, strong Assam to eliminate the jitters brought on by a three-cup-a-day coffee overdose ~ or the sleeplessness that comes with a poorly timed macchiato. (Both green and black teas contain caffeine, but this amount is typically less than half that of a cup of coffee ~ making it suitable for those who find themselves at the mercy of caffeine highs and lows.)

Tea is a completely different animal; instead of instant gratification, it's a drink to linger over ~ not with a book on the couch, but, increasingly, at the best cafes. Tegan Godwin is just one twenty-something who's traded her signature soy cap for green tea or chai at her regular weekend brunches with girlfriends. And she wants the real deal brewed with milk, not a latte made with syrup or powder: "It's not real tea," she says. "I also don't like the cheaper paper some brands use for tea bags; I can taste it," she adds. The new wave of tea drinkers want café culture and they want character: exotic infusions, organic loose-leaf and high-quality single-estate teas to satisfy sophisticated palates ~ and their numbers are only growing.

(Opposite) Image supplied by The Oriental Tea House.

A Healthy Knowledge

Tea may be the new (long) black, but this revival is about much more than just chucking jigglers into a mug. "Tea certainly has the strength to stand on its own merits, but people are rediscovering tea and going deeper to understand it," says tea purveyor Arthur Tong of Sydney's Tea Craft, which services fine restaurants such as Tetsuya's and Claude's, and cafés including Brasserie Bread and Not Bread Alone.

"There's a renaissance of loose-leaf tea drinking and appreciation in the past few years," he adds. "This may be in part due to the slow food movement and, in general, Australians' seriousness when it comes to good food and wellbeing."

The high antioxidant levels in green tea have become common knowledge, but recent studies into black tea are revealing it can be equally good for you, points out naturopath Mim Beim, who has developed her own range of therapeutic tea blends, Beaming With Health, and is a champion of tea's health benefits. These range, she says, from boosting immunity to lowering the stress hormone cortisol. "Studies have shown that drinking three cups of tea a day helps decrease the risk of heart disease and some cancers. One particular study showed that men and women who drank one or more cups of tea (black or green) had a 44 per cent reduction in heart attack risk compared to those who didn't drink tea," she adds.

Cultural Exchange

The Aussie tea drinker is fast gaining an appreciation for different varieties, and is developing a more seasoned palate. We can buy fine and exotic teas and know how to make them well at home, so if we're in a café or restaurant, there's now an expectation of getting something special.

"Tea drinkers, like coffee drinkers, are a fussy bunch," says Tea Master Tjok Gde Kerthyasa, Arthur Tong's partner at Tea Craft. "They like their tea served properly, with thoughtfulness and respect." Thankfully, many cafés and restaurants are starting to take tea as seriously as their coffee ~ and the rest of their produce, for that matter. A limp tea bag just isn't going to cut it anymore.

The humble bag can't be ruled out entirely, however. Often criticised for containing lesser-grade teas and having a short shelf life due to the small leaf size, there are tea bags that have made leaps and bounds to combine convenience and quality. With the aim of making good tea easy to achieve in the fast pace of a café (or when you're too lazy to use a teapot at home), companies such as Tea Drop and Chamellia Organic Fair Trade Tea are using pyramid-shaped nylon-mesh and muslin bags that are large enough to allow space for tea leaves to unfurl — which produces a finer flavour and aroma. Two Leaves and a Bud takes the pyramid teabag even further: its organic whole-leaf teas are contained in bags made of biodegradable cornstarch-based nylon.

Don't assume, however, that all tea is equal; the way it's been sourced and prepared will come through in the cup. Arthur explains: "Our boutique coffee colleagues take what they do very seriously. They go about sourcing the best beans and roasting them in a way that characterises their personality to offer people something unique. What we do with our tea is very similar; we taste and select the best, and we craft blends with our own hands so we know exactly what goes into it."

Finally, when it comes to the way tea is served, we're all praying for the day scorched sencha is nothing but a bad memory. Serious punters such as Melbourne's Proud Mary will use a thermometer to ensure it's done right, but for discerning tea lovers in search of quality,

Nathan Wakeford of Chamellia Organic Fair Trade Tea offers these tips: "Ask yourself, 'Does the cafe communicate through its tea menu, signage or verbally, the name of the tea estate; its region and elevation; the grade of leaf; its certifications; the date of plucking and the lot number?' When it comes to buying tea, ask your purveyor if they have travelled to the estates, if they know the peak flavour period to source the tea with the best character and quality from a particular region, or if they can explain the factors that designate leaf quality and faults in manufacture."

Gone are the days when you'd be better off buying your own loose leaf and making it at home. But, as Tjok says, "Tea culture is continually evolving in Australia," and perhaps the best is yet to come.

Find your
T~SPOT

Sydney

The Tea Room Gunners Barracks
End Of Suakin Drive, Mosman

Maximus Cafe
GPO Building, 1 Martin Place

Artos Espresso
Lobby, 233 Castlereigh Street

Bird Cow Fish
500 Crown Street, Surry Hills

The Bunker
399 Liverpool Street, Darlinghurst

Cafe Ish
82 Campbell Street, Surry Hills

Melbourne

Hopetoun Tea Rooms
The Block, 282 Collins Street

Caffe e Cucina
581 Chapel Street, South Yarra

Carlton Espresso
326 Carlton Street, Carlton

Monk Bodhi Dharma
Rear 202 Carlisle Street, Balaclava

Nabiha
10 Hall Street, Moonee Ponds

Espresso Elements
305 Hampton Street, Hampton

J'adore Cafe
504 Centre Road, Bentleigh

Cups on the go
to warm up your sales

Double walled paper hot cups from Huhtamaki surpass all other paper cups in looks, performance and quality. With its new universal lid to fit all three cup sizes, better insulation, and quality food grade paper, it gives you advantages you can see and feel.

For a premium on-the-go hot drink experience you will enjoy safely, contact Huhtamaki Australia on **1800 043 584** or www.huhtamaki.com

HUHTAMAKI

ODD SPOT
302 Melbourne Street, Newport

Eclectic and cosy is probably the best way to sum up the Odd Spot. This reasonably priced cafe, sharing space with only two other shops and a minor take away chain is indeed in an odd spot on the main drag of Newport. Its charm and warmth are matched by the way the staff make you feel immediately at home.

The menu has plenty of variety, and it's difficult to make a decision. In the end I settle for some simple, thick fruit toast, which comes with a selection of jams and preserves.

My espresso has a light, even crema, and a pleasing aroma with a slight nutty presence. A delicate mouthfeel is balanced by caramel that dances on the tongue, ending in a smooth hazelnut finish. The latte is a bit more of a mixed bag. The addition of milk tends to mute those wonderful, complex caramel notes, but the way it combines with the coffee's lovely nutty finish is near perfection.

Phone
+613 9399 2241

Trading Hours
everyday: 8am - 4pm

Cafe... 19/25
Coffee... 19/25
Di Bella Coffee

WOODSTOCK ESPRESSO BAR
1150 High Street, Armadale

This stylish cafe slips effortlessly in among Armadale's antique stores, designer clothing and chic homewares shops. You enter through a large, archway to an entirely more modern and minimalist interior. Simple table settings spill out into a large outdoor area, perfect for people-watching in the sun.

The Saturday brunch peak has the place buzzing with cyclists, real estate types and fashionable young things. A cool-looking crew of baristas mans a large La Marzocco at the back of the cafe. The waitstaff are a tad too cool (and disengaged), and there's a mix up in my coffee order.

Fortunately, the standard of coffee is unencumbered by the cool. My espresso looks the part, and affects a sophisticated, spicy aroma. The coffee is a little over-heated but delivers on flavour — roasted mixed nuts and dark chocolate. An elegant acidity and tenacious texture ensure the luscious Lindt finish is long. If only the service were as serious as the coffee! I hope they pull up their socks — if they're wearing any…

Phone
+613 9500 1483

Trading Hours
everyday winter:
7am - 5pm
everyday summer:
7am - 10pm

Cafe... 19/25
Coffee... 19/25
5 Senses Coffee

PENNY FARTHING ESPRESSO
206 High Street, Northcote

Proving that old-fashioned style can harmonise with modern sensibilities, nattily dressed brothers Steve and Trevor (love the braces, guys) deliver this recently-opened pitstop to Northcote.

There's plenty to like here, from the namesake bicycle in the window, to the whitewashed walls and comfortable scatter of wooden tables. While some may find the all-day breakfast menu light on options, the serves are generous, with a strong focus on quality organic and locally-sourced produce (we particularly like the feta and avocado smash on sourdough with a side of fresh chilli). Lunch offerings include hearty salads and sangers, like the inspired chicken, celery and walnut with homemade mayo.

But it's the coffee that really packs a punch. The house blend delivers a subtle nutty aroma that gives way to a surprisingly tongue-tingling brew. Big on acidity and mouthfeel, its finish is short and sharp. With milk, the nuttiness is accentuated, resulting in a velvety smooth coffee that loses none of its kick. Well worth crossing town for.

Phone
+613 9482 2246

Trading Hours
tue - fri: 7.30am - 4pm
sat - sun: 8.30am - 5pm
monday closed

Cafe... 22/25
Coffee... 23/25
5 Senses Coffee

CAFE LE CHIEN
3 Gamon Street, Seddon

Okay, so we know that Seddon is one of the hotspots west of the River, where Melbournians of a certain age migrate when they want to spread out in affordable (for now) tranquillity. Le Chien is the type of place that wouldn't have been found here so many years ago. It caters resolutely to the new mood of Seddon, and it does it well.

The front windows are a great spot to catch some late-afternoon sun while you sip your cuppa Joe. The décor is engagingly inner-city and the service is cheery despite the lunchtime rush. Word about these parts is that this is the best coffee around. You'll just have to work your way through *The Coffee Guide* to prove it true, but it certainly is a good drop.

The espresso is well extracted, with a choc-biscuit aroma and good, velvet consistency. Berry and citrus on the palate, mine is a little earthy — but not to its detriment. Try the affogato: it's first class, and eases the pain of rising real estate.

Phone
+613 9362 7333

Trading Hours
sun - tue: 8am - 3pm
wed - sat: 8am - 10pm

Cafe... 18/25
Coffee... 18/25
Coffee Supreme

Outer Melbourne

STUDIO MOVIDA
138 Cotham Road, Kew

Concerned that your full-cream milk lattes are sitting a little heavy on the hips? Here's the solution: In addition to crafting a very nicely extracted espresso, Studio Movida has adjoining facilities where you can work it off with a spin class, a Pilates session, or even a massage to ease the aches and pains.

Make no mistake though, the cafe is no afterthought. These guys take their caffeine seriously. The house blend Veneziano is a perfectly enjoyable, choc-caramel affair with a velvety texture and mild, short finish. It's well made, with an ochre crema and a light toast aroma.

It's a mark of the maturation of Melbourne's coffee culture that such a well-made example can be found in Kew. The real joy, however, lies in the ever-changing bean-of-the-day brew. Reading like an airport destination board to exotic locales, the daily advertised single-estate beans from parts far-flung are well worth some exploration.

Phone
+613 9817 4954

Trading Hours
mon - fri: 7am - 5pm
sat - sun: 8am - 3pm

Cafe... 17/25
Coffee... 18/25
Veneziano

PALOMINO
236 High Street, Northcote

This Northcote coffee house's fit-out might not win awards for originality – think a coarse, exposed concrete floor, white-painted lining-board ceiling and quaintly retro op-shop nick-nacks – and its occasionally aloof staff might not endear themselves to the clientele, but Palomino has a little something that keeps locals coming back.

Perhaps it's the cute and often inventive menu; highlights include a piquant meatball roll with pecorino pepato, and a sweet bruschetta of brioche and ricotta infused with honey and cinnamon. Perhaps it's the great view from the window seats of the diverse High Street foot traffic (middle-aged punk; twenty-something urban hipster; yummy mummy with iPhone and Bugaboo). Or perhaps it's just the sense of familiarity engendered by the inner-northern cafe formula

As fo my coffee, its texture is creamy, its aroma brings on caramel and chocolate, and its mellow sweetness is lifted by a faint hint of acidity.

Phone
+613 9481 0699

Trading Hours
mon - sat: 8am - 4.30pm
sun: 9am - 4.30pm

Cafe... 18/25
Coffee... 21/25
Palomino Blend

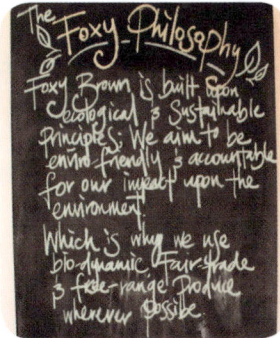

FOXY BROWN ESPRESSO
31a South Crescent, Northcote

Owner/Barista Pat Sloane is the energy behind Foxy Brown, and from the second you place your order he's attentive to every detail. Pat works hard to keep Foxy up to his exacting standards, and it pays off. The long space is full of '70s retro charm — all orange and brown, it makes you want to melt into the front-porch couch and just let the kids run amok.

There's a coffee menu detailing the flavour profiles of what's on offer (fair trade and organic), and of course a variety of take-home options including Foxy's own espresso blend.

After Pat talks me through the selection of soy milks he's been working with since "Bonsoy-gate", my latte arrives with cascading layers in the glass, full of nuts and cocoa tones. It's a mellow start to the day, easing me into Foxy's espresso, which is dark with smoky chocolate, and enjoys a happy little citrus kick to get me on my way. Sure is "the best damn brown in town"!

Phone
+613 9481 4454

Trading Hours
everyday: 8am - 5pm

Cafe... 21/25
Coffee... 23/25
Foxy Brown Blend

Outer Melbourne

MJ FORTY CAFE & BAR
40 Nicholson Street, Essendon

Set in a quiet pocket of Essendon, MJ Forty is a great little place to escape the intricacies of life. Spread over many rooms of an old, brick house, this popular cafe serves an array of dishes from bacon and eggs to pastas and homemade biscuits and cakes — and chef/owner Michael Neagle adds specials to the menu on a regular basis.

Outdoor tables adorn the main entrance while the front room oozes sunlight and is a hub for mothers and kids from nearby schools. For those wanting a little more privacy, the cafe's back rooms and rear courtyard are perfect for reading the newspaper or for intimate gatherings with friends.

Although some aspects of the venue appear a little outdated, the same cannot be said for the coffee, which is superb. My espresso is smooth in body, its sour flavour balanced out by a sweet, long aftertaste. My cappuccino's chocolaty aroma is the ideal wake-up call, with its velvety, mild taste leaving a pleasant trail on the palate.

Phone
+613 9326 2966

Trading Hours
mon - wed: 8am - 5pm
thur - sun: 8am - 6pm

Cafe... 18/25
Coffee... 17/25
Tonino Lamborghini

VYVE CAFE
184 Burgundy Street, Heidelberg

There's something of a bar feel to this Heidelberg cafe. But then, it serves up Atomica coffee with a note advising that brewing temperatures are kept warm (rather than hot) for the benefit of the bean — so you suspect you're in good hands.

You can cosy-up on a plush armchair to watch the bustle of the street outside, but if there's work to do, you won't feel out of place at a table with your laptop. There's a sense that Vyve can be anything you want it to be: breakfast spot, lunch haunt, dinner or drinks venue — and the grey tones and muted lighting are equally accommodating.

A soy latte is pleasantly nutty and creamy, but my espresso intrudes with strong notes of burnt caramel and roasted peanuts, before rolling thickly around the mouth and finishing with a soft acidity. And it's especially comforting to have a good coffee on hand no matter what the time of day.

Phone
+613 9458 2222

Trading Hours
tue: 7.30am - 5pm
wed - thur: 7.30am - 10.30pm
fri - sat: 7.30am - 11pm
sun: 8am - 5pm
monday closed

Cafe... 19/25
Coffee... 19/25
Atomica

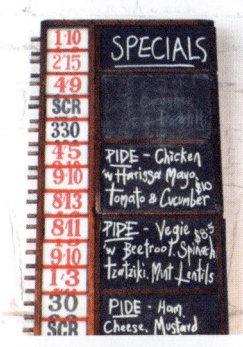

THE CORNERSHOP
11 Ballarat Street, Yarraville

Every suburb needs a Cornershop. With its blend of European style and boho chic, this friendly local manages a perfect balance between urban sophistication and homey appeal, making us want to uproot to Yarraville posthaste.

There's much to like, from the seating (communal table, window bar or sunny courtyard), to the efficient staff, Mediterranean-inspired menu and amusing quirky touches (specials are listed on a bookie's tote board, while a chamber pot collects tips).

My single-origin espresso arrives quickly, though appears a tad under-extracted. However, the bright citric acidity is complemented by a fruitiness reminiscent of oranges and toast, making it the perfect accompaniment to a decadent raspberry muffin. It's a smooth drop, with a finish that lingers on the tip of the tongue. The addition of milk mutes the flavour somewhat, but the new level of sweetness makes the latte a fitting brew for daydreaming over the property pages.

Phone
+613 9689 0052

Trading Hours
mon: 8am - 5pm
tue - sat: 8am - 10pm
sun: 8am - 4pm

Cafe... 19/25
Coffee... 18/25
Coffee Supreme

Outer Melbourne

WILD TOAST
234 High Street, Kew

Until recently, High Street in Kew has been a bit of a cafe non-event. Enter Wild Toast, with it's charm and attention to detail, and things look set to change. From the crazy collection of crockery (think pre-loved Shelly tea-cups as sugar bowls) and the artwork from Bird's Gallery next door, to a menu that boasts some of the best baked-beans in town, it's clear the team here has really stepped up to the plate. Big chunky wooden tables invite you in, while jars of homemade jam and chutney might accompany you home.

The coffee is Toby's Estate, fair trade and organic, and the cheery baristas are always up for a chinwag. But despite the chitchat, decafs and cappuccinos roll out in good time. My espresso is a little watery, but it's hot and earthy with a medium finish, and sets me up nicely for the heavy, creamy latte that follows. A great mix of good coffee and easy charm on a formerly forlorn strip.

Phone
+613 9855 0555

Trading Hours
mon - fri: 7.30am - 4.30pm
sat - sun: 7.30am - 4pm

Cafe... 19/25
Coffee... 18/25
Toby's Estate

TRULY SCRUMPTIOUS
Shop 4, Granary Lane, Mentone

One of the great things about Melbourne is that brilliant coffee has spread to the suburbs. Truly Scrumptious is testament to this.

I'm enthusiastically greeted by the barista as I enter, and as I make myself comfortable on a sofa bench in the main room, my attention is diverted by the offerings of a massive blackboard on the wall: home-made lemon tarts, vanilla slices, chocolate fudge cake and sweet and savoury muffins. Lunch specials, which include Spanish paella and a smoked salmon linguine with champagne cream sauce, are a cut above your suburban average.

My espresso's aroma foreshadows its exotic spice, which is well-matched with a punchy acidity and solid body. I follow with a latte which, disappointingly, is over-hot. Once cooled, it's a pleasant cup, with the milk drawing luscious caramel, chocolate and nut flavours from the Giancarlo beans. Great to get out of the city for a solid coffee.

Phone
+613 9584 9907

Trading Hours
mon - fri: 8am - 4pm
sat: 8am - 2pm
sunday closed

Cafe... 18/25
Coffee... 19/25
Giancarlo By Grinders

CORNELIUS
141 Maling Road, Canterbury

This Canterbury provedore has its sights set on spreading the "life is tasty" word. And Cornelius is a feast for the senses, with everything from cheese displays of blues and goats, to wine, crackers and specialist sweets — absinthe sucker, anyone?

Aside from the cold counter and open kitchen – which churns out the famous cheesy toast – there's a scattering of tables where you can rewrite the shopping list over a locally roasted brew. The coffee here is a varying blend, roasted for Cornelius by the Maling Room just up the road. The beans are never more than a week old from roasting when served, and the flavour varies subtly with every batch.

Today, my espresso arrives pungent with resinous chocolaty aromas. It washes over the tongue like smooth, mellow velvet, before finishing with a surprising brightness and light acidity. You might not get the same coffee twice, but it's always good. After all, as Anna (the La Marzocco wrangler) puts it: "What is extraordinary produce without extraordinary coffee to back it up?"

Phone
+613 9830 7915

Trading Hours
mon - sat: 8am - 5pm
sun: 9am - 4pm

Cafe... 21/25
Coffee... 19/25
Cornelius Blend

SEDDON DEADLY SINS
148 Victoria Street, Seddon

Of a weekend, the denizens of Melbourne's inner west flock to Seddon Deadly Sins' sun-dappled and leafy courtyard — and who can blame them? The place is charming. Staff flit about and wait tables with consummate efficiency, bantering wittily all the while. They hand out delightful menus covered with recycled Little Golden Books. And they take their coffee seriously (Metro beans are used here). What's not to love?

My espresso is bright, with a hazelnut tang, and is long on the palate. Although a little watery, it's robust on the nose with strident tobacco and earthy notes. The latte – served at the perfect temperature – is smooth and caramel-like, with citrus and cinnamon. Both beverages team perfectly with our shared plate of pancakes topped with bananas and drizzled with caramel sauce.

For those who inhabit the other pages of the Melways, Seddon Deadly Sins is well worth the drive over the bridge. Pick a sunny day.

Phone
+613 9689 3092

Trading Hours
tue - sun: 8am - 5pm
monday closed

Cafe... 16/25
Coffee... 20/25
Metro Coffee

Outer Melbourne

FEEDBACK CAFE
31 Ballarat Street, Yarraville

The Yarraville cafe scene is one of the most over-serviced in the inner city. But Feedback Cafe more than holds its own, having garnered a loyal local following. The retro-styled interior – coloured plastic chandelier, Laminex tables and vintage crockery – is welcoming, and the noticeboard is full of community flyers. There's a good stock of well-loved children's books, but prams would be a squeeze in this small space.

The breakfast and lunch menu offers hearty, sustaining food, with plenty of vegetarian options. But the coffee alone is enough for a visit. A spicy, woody aroma wafts from the espresso, with its golden-brown crema. It's a delight to sip the smooth brew, which leaves a lovely, soft aftertaste lingering on the palate. The latte, decorated with a well-executed rosetta, has no discernable aroma, but it's sweet, creamy and enjoyable to sip. Little wonder Feedback is a hit with the locals.

Phone
+613 9689 1955

Trading Hours
mon - fri: 7.30am - 3.30pm
sat: 8am - 2.30pm
sun: 8.30am - 2.30pm

Cafe... 18/25
Coffee... 17/25
Allpress Espresso

POD ESPRESSO
305 Bay Street, Brighton

Aptly named, this cosy cafe with its high-traffic coffee-dispensing window on North Brighton train station is a cocoon-like haven. It is not, we were relieved to discover, named for coffee's interpretation of the tea bag; the Veneziano coffee is freshly ground *à la minute*.

With just a few indoor tables nestled side-by-side, the boundaries of social space are quickly invaded by a communal eating free for all. Stylishly clean lines are softened by earthy tones and lampshade lighting, with the sweet smell of home-baked muffins and the gurglings of a majestic La Marzocco in all her three-group glory. Trains' bells and whistles fade out of earshot, unless you're seated at the more generous smattering of kerbside tables.

A very short, oily espresso borders on a ristretto. Its floral, chocolate aroma is a precursor to an intense hit, quickly mellowed by the pleasant bitterness of dark chocolate. The aftertaste is long and harmonious — and nicely balanced like peas in a pod.

Trading Hours
mon - fri: 6am - 4pm
sat: 6am - 2pm
sun: 7am - 2.30pm

Cafe... 17/25
Coffee... 19/25
Veneziano

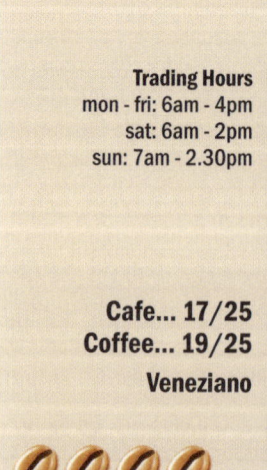

DUCHESS OF SPOTSWOOD
87 Hudsons Road, Spotswood

With a peerage-inspired name and *Country Style* décor (think crystal chandelier, polished boards and pastel ceiling), you'd be forgiven for thinking this place is a little bit posh. Instead, the friendly staff, tiny open kitchen and touches like the honesty-system fruit bowl create a laid-back atmosphere, perfect for chilling with the weekend papers.

The menu, too, is unpretentious. Anglophiles will rejoice at the range of British favourites, including black pudding, gentlemen's relish and cream of cauliflower soup. The Breakfast of Champignons is a standout: a tumble of sautéed mushrooms on thickly cut Zealy Bay toast. Whatever your choice, follow it up with a slab of sticky treacle tart — yummo.

Given the British penchant for tea, the Duchess's coffee is surprisingly good. The espresso (delivered in cute pastel china) has a subtle toffee aroma and thick caramel crema. Nippy on the tongue, with a buttery mouthfeel, it leaves a short, sweet aftertaste. With milk, the acidity is mellowed, resulting in a lighter, but super creamy drop. Delightful.

Phone
+613 9391 6016

Trading Hours
mon - fri: 7am - 4.30pm
sat - sun: 8am - 4pm

Cafe... 21/25
Coffee... 20/25
**Candy Man Blend
By Small Batch**

Outer Melbourne

The Alchemist challenge

They gather in their secret laboratories sorting, grinding, mixing and brewing. When they think they have created their special potion, they let the boiled liquid cool slowly, they then stir and separate the thousands of solid particles, they take a loud slurp of the liquid gold, sucking air around the warm liquid to enhance the hundreds of flavours. They then hold the brew in their mouths, swirling around looking for a creeping in of taste profiles as they try to separate the different nuances experienced.

Without swallowing any of the magical brew, they spit out the concoction and step back for a moment to let the 10,000 taste buds go wild in their mouths as they search for the unique flavours that has been let loose and running wild on their palates. Flavours that have not yet ever been tasted go spinning through the minds of these chosen individuals like fireworks on New Years Eve.

But they are all still waiti[ng] for the big bang to go off [in] their mouths all searching f[or] flavour nirvana, the ultimate taste sensation.

Yes they are alchemist chemist wizards, and they come from a specialised group of professionals called "The Coffee Roaster".

This process happens everyday in th[e] life of a coffee roaster. They not only roast many different origins of coffee beans, they also need the combined skill[s] of cupping the brew to find the final flavo[ur] that will differentiate them from the rest of [the pack.]

Coffee flavours are determined by many variables such as the country of origin, coffee type and botanical species, the farming process, the soil types, altitude of the crop and the way the bean is then picked. Then there is the processing which can change flavours dramatically, with the difference between the quick wet processing of coffee beans to the longer sun drying methods. The roaster then has the challenge of the roasting process itself, knowing what colour profile to take the bean to, to get the most out of it for its particular brewing method. Then once roasted the roaster then goes through the trial and error of blending, trying to finish with a blend that will be their trademark in the competitive industry.

In Australia there are over 350 coffee roasting companies that are supplying the billion dollar consumer market nation wide. All the roasters in Australia were looking for a point of difference to compete in this very competitive marketplace. Until a few years back there was no real regulative base where coffee roasters could gather and share their experiences. There were a few regional agricultural shows that had small areas for coffee roasters to enter but they were not accepted by the sceptical industry as credible places to showcase the skills of this group. Then four years ago seasoned coffee and cafe communicators KISS Marketing got involved and created a competition where all the coffee roasters of Australia could come together and compete on an educational format with their skills. Not only can they participate as judges of the event looking at their industry peers but they can learn by networking with fellow roasters on neutral ground.

The CSR Golden Bean Competition

The Golden Bean Roasters Competition was first run in 2006 with around one hundred roasters involved. Sweetener Company Equal contributed with sponsorship making the event possible. The event organizer, KISS Marketing under the direction of Sean Edward had the challenge of getting the right blend of coffee companies to participate and the right group of professional baristas to present the coffee in its best format on the top of the line brewing equipment. Sean recognised that the coffee industry had to be represented as a whole and had categories for all sections of the industry including, cafe franchise and retail. With this, judges used different brewing methods to bring out the best of these specialist roasted coffees.

The Golden Bean now in its forth year attracts over seven hundred entries from Australia's 350 coffee roasters making this one of the biggest roasting competitions in the world. The event now has a major sponsor with CSR Sugar becoming involved. This year's winning roaster for 2009/2010 was Di Bella Coffee, a national coffee roaster that originates from Brisbane. The team from Di Bella were part of the one hundred roasters who participated in the event in the coastal resort town of Port Macquarie, NSW. Master Roaster Anne Cooper was at the ready to except the trophy and the honour of being the best at her craft amongst her peers. Company Principle, Phillip Di Bella gave an inspirational speech to the caffeine primed audience about passion and people. Phillip is no newcomer to success having created one of the fastest growing coffee businesses in the country and a winner of the young businesses people's award.

...ent organiser Sean Edwards from KISS Marketing was overwhelmed by the entries ...this years event with over 700 hundred coffees entered in seven categories. The ...offees were tested over the weekend being made by world class barista champions, ...avid Makin and Tim Adams both Australian champion baristas. The judges at the event ...ere a selection of coffee roasters, international green bean brokers and coffee growers. ...e event was head judged by Justin Metcalf the head judge for the World Barista ...ampionships and Head Roaster for Daily Roast.

...e CSR Golden Bean also hosted educational seminars looking at Marketing, Green Bean ...ocurement and Roaster Maintenance. The Key Note speaker was the passionate Geoff ...atts from Intelligentsia a third wave coffee business out of America. Geoff took the ...en audience through his journey of the new third wave coffee movement looking at the ...hical trends within the coffee industry and how roasters can support the third world ...ffee growing nations.

...SS Marketing is looking forward to a bigger event next year 2010/2011 and getting the ...ll support from all the 350 coffee roasters in Australia. With the help of major sponsors ...ch as CSR the 8.5 billion dollar coffee industry can now reward its main contributors ...r their efforts in growing this exciting industry. The winners receive gold, silver and ...onze medals in the seven categories with the overall winners of the CSR Golden Bean ...ing the highest score between the milk based and espresso categories.
...e 2010 competition will be focusing on getting more roasters to the event so the event ...ganisers can get a clear picture of where the industry wants to head with its growth and prosperity.

So, soon it will be time again for those roasters to get on their white coats and re-enter their laboratories and come up with the perfect brew.

For more information visit **www.cafebiz.net**
or call **02 6583 7163**

CAFFE ROMEO
319 Doncaster Road, Balwyn North

Caffe Romeo shows why cafes, like books, and possibly even people, shouldn't be judged by appearances. Hidden away in the corner of a nondescript suburban shopping strip, Romeo relies on word of mouth rather than flash décor or splashy architecture. And the word around town is that the coffee here is good – very good – and beloved by locals.

Run by Italian-born coffee purist Stefano and his wife Vicky, the focus is unashamedly on coffee. There's no menu (just a few pastries), but the place is always busy. Coffee is roasted in house, in a Ferrari-red roaster, and the premium house blend is created from an international selection primarily from South America.

The short black is an easy-sipping example of a great espresso: a fruity, floral aroma; gentle and sweet on the palate. The latte is a harmonious blend of a slightly nutty coffee base with smooth, creamy milk. Appearances be damned — Romeo is winning hearts.

Phone
+613 9857 6444

Trading Hours
mon - fri: 7.30am - 5pm
sat: 7.30am - 3.30pm
sunday closed

Cafe... 19/25
Coffee... 21/25
Caffe Romeo

CAFE WHYTE
1122 Glenhuntly Road, Glenhuntly

Quiet and restrained, with modern art on the walls and long benches, Cafe Whyte's relaxed atmosphere is a terrific place to unwind. Timber blinds and the wood floor add homely touches. The furniture has a well-used feel, and the acoustic music on the stereo is so relaxing I could lay down on a bench and snooze.

The menu is standard cafe fare, with a large breakfast selection, burgers, salads, and Turkish breads. There are a few stand-outs, such as the Creole Chicken Curry and Prawn Wonton Short Soup. The staff are friendly and attentive without being intrusive. They keep a keen eye from a distance, only popping forward occasionally to refill my glass of water.

My espresso has a solid, light brown crema. Delving deeper, woody flavours are balanced, mid-palate, with medium acidity. A short, sharp yet pleasing finish rounds out the shot. The latte is well extracted, but slightly marred by overheated milk, giving up some of its much-needed sweetness.

Phone
+613 9569 2212

Trading Hours
mon - sat: 7.30am - 5pm
sun: 9am - 5pm

Cafe... 21/25
Coffee... 17/25
Di Bella Coffee

The *Classic* Italian Icon

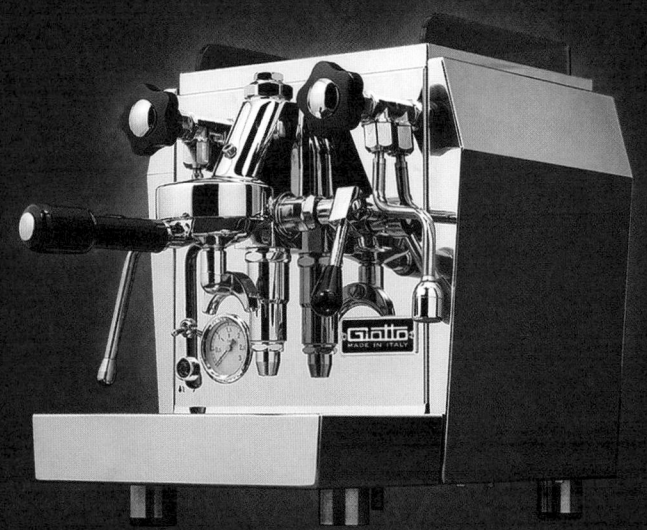

...ocket Espresso is pleased to announce the release of the new Giotto ...omestic espresso machine. Our research and development together ...ith international customer feedback has led to our new machine ...eing developed in the tradition of quality that is Giotto; offering a premium domestic espresso machine to those passionate about creating the finest espresso possible at home.

New Machine Features • New steam and hot water handles • New control panel safety features • New and redesigned feet for ...creased height and stability • New slide drain tray with elegant contours • Commercial pressures stat for longevity • Thicker stronger cup frame surround • New heavy duty pressure gauge • Larger and newly configured Thermosyphon System for greater temperature control and stability to the group; while optimising steam quality

Creating classic espresso machines

www.giotto.com.au   1300 326 326   espresso company AUSTRALIA

HAUSFRAU
32a Ballarat Street, Yarraville

For the domestically-challenged, Hausfrau is a godsend. This cute-as-a-button bakery specialises in home-style goodies which are perfect for passing off as your own. And there's plenty to choose from: the changing display – heavily influenced by the owner's Austrian heritage – sports everything from jammy Linzer tortes to caramelised onion scrolls. We particularly love the mini chocolate cakes topped with rosebuds.

In keeping with all things domestic goddess, the décor is pastel-toned, creating a soothing atmosphere for the largely yummy-mummy clientele. Giant enamel water pitchers and large floral lightshades add a certain country feel.

My espresso, with its dark caramel crema and smoky aroma, has a strong, tarry flavour and good acidity but lacks the mouthfeel I'd expect. It also seems a trifle burnt — a bad day on the coffee machine perhaps? All is forgiven, however, when I try the latte. Super-creamy, its mild acidity is supported by delicate chocolate undertones, resulting in a sweet, lingering finish — just the thing for another run at the cake display.

Phone
+613 9687 8364

Trading Hours
tue - sun: 9am - 5pm
monday closed

Cafe... 17/25
Coffee... 17/25
Genovese Coffee

IZZI ESPRESSO
272 Glenhuntly Road, Elsternwick

Located conveniently near Elsternwick railway station, this tiny bolthole in a busy shopping strip only has enough seating for about six people; however, there's a steady trade in takeaways. If you decide to sit in, take note of the clever upholstery on the bench seating — made from recycled coffee sacks!

The Gravity espresso is not particularly complex, and comes across as a little thin, but it has a pleasant sweet-cigar flavour, if a rather muted aroma. The finish is short but bitey, and overall the coffee is clean on the palate. The latte is a competent brew with a baked-bread aroma and very good crema. It has a silky texture and is served at just the right temperature.

Food options are limited to a small selection of filled rolls and pastries, which the cheerful staff will explain to you. Grab the papers, and a window seat, and watch the locals trundle by.

Phone
+613 9528 1370

Trading Hours
mon - fri: 6am - 4.30pm
sat: 6am - 3.30pm
sunday closed

Cafe... 15/25
Coffee... 14/25
Gravity Coffee

RUPERT & THE FIG
300 Bay Street, Brighton

The guys at Rupert & the Fig place a whole lot of importance on knowing where their produce comes from, and the menu here comes complete with some light reading about suppliers. The bread is from Dench, the eggs are Green and the milk is Demeter — a producer A-list if ever there were one. So it's little wonder they roast their own coffee, to ensure it's a worthy stablemate.

The espresso suggests as much. Tingly and trumpeting citrusy notes up front, it's a piquant and bright little buzz in the cup, rusty looking with a long and satisfying finish. A latte, to accompany some fruit toast, is a little on the weak side, but sweet and mellow with a smooth finish.

Currently the guys are roasting their own beans with a friend's equipment, but rumour has it they'll be opening another joint soon, affording the room to run the whole show themselves.

Watch this space.

Phone
+613 9596 4047

Trading Hours
mon - fri: 7am - 5pm
sat - sun: 8am - 5pm

Cafe... 19/25
Coffee... 19/25
Rupert & the Fig

Outer Melbourne

THREAD CAFE
1373 Malvern Road, Malvern

From the outset, Thread exudes a passion for food and family. It's only been open for a month at the time of this review, but we're already liking the modern hard surfaces softened by enchanting homely touches. There's also an Egyptian theme that subtly weaves its way through the cafe, which may all sound cluttered and confused, but it works.

The Egyptian/Mediterranean theme comes to the fore in the menu, with pide and Egyptian Happy Eggs. Much of the menu consists of items served with lashings of feta, dukkah, or honey, and others soaked in rosewater. Care has been taken in balancing flavours and using high-quality ingredients.

My espresso has a dark-speckled crema and smells of subtle spice. The flavour maintains the spice and enjoys a pleasant acidity, which rounds out wonderfully to a smooth toffee finish, rolling over the tongue. My latte is well balanced, mild, with a finish that combines toffee and milk together in harmony. A promising start for this uncommon Thread.

Phone
+613 9822 8668

Trading Hours
tue - fri: 7.30am - 4pm
sat - sun: 8.30am - 4pm
monday closed

Cafe... 20/25
Coffee... 18/25
Allpress Espresso

CRUNCH CAFE
669 High Street, Thornbury

It's not easy to build character into a new cafe occupying an old shopfront, but the team at Crunch has managed it with aplomb. The concrete and timber interior is minimalist without being alienating; the nick nacks are cute but not kitsch; the open kitchen provides colour and movement; and the floor-to-ceiling glass that opens onto High Street offers a neatly framed view of passing foot traffic and a leafy side-street beyond. What's more, the place has a buzzing energy, especially on weekend mornings.

But that comes as no surprise: lingering over a couple of pieces of lightly toasted sourdough dripping with zesty orange and tamarind marmalade, all washed down with a steaming latte, is arguably the best way to start the day this side of Separation Street. The coffee here offers subtle berry aromas and hints of savoury spice. The mouthfeel is light but palate-coating, and well-balanced flavours of nutmeg and pepper are revealed in the lengthy aftertaste. You can't ask for more character than that.

Phone
+613 9495 1565

Trading Hours
tue- fri: 7.30am - 3pm
sat - sun: 8am - 3pm
monday closed

Cafe... 16/25
Coffee...18/25
Atomica

Main Photograph kindly provided by Espresso Elements

ESPRESSO ELEMENTS
305 Hampton Street, Hampton

True to its name, this place is all about the fundamentals of espresso. It sells espresso machines, coffee accessories, fresh-roasted blends and exotic syrups, as well as java by the cup for immediate consumption. Don't come here looking for a slap-up breakfast — food is limited to a small selection of sweet treats.

This place is in the heart of the Hampton shopping strip, close to the station, and does a good job of keeping the local bayside crowd perky and refreshed. We note that besides demonstrating and selling a range of coffee machines, the shop also offers servicing and repairs. There's also a range of drinking chocolates and teas.

Our efficient barista serves up a very quaffable espresso that's nutty and sweet, albeit a little watery and quite short on the palate. It's a fine heart-starter nonetheless, made from the El Salvador Organic blend of the week. The latte boasts an excellent crema and rich, creamy consistency which conveys a fruity, spicy flavour and almond and toffee aroma.

Phone
+613 9597 0262

Trading Hours
mon - fri: 7am - 5pm
sat - sun: 8am - 5pm

Cafe... **18/25**
Coffee... **18/25**
Espresso Elements

Outer Melbourne

COCO LOUNGE
93 Kingsway, Glen Waverley

Polished concrete floors, neutral colours and dark woods set the scene at Coco Lounge. Old-school posters are high on the walls, and the ceiling fans are working overtime to keep the heat at bay. The Lounge is well positioned to scoop up movie-goers looking for a bite to eat — or a drink afterwards in the upstairs bar.

The menu has all-day breakfast choices served with Phillippa's breads. Pizza, pasta and risotto make a showing, as do generous mains like the Italian Burger and Steak Sandwich. Included is a coffee menu that concentrates on syrups and additives, rather than different ways of serving espresso, and there's a selection of wines and beers.

My espresso arrives quickly and has a light brown, even crema. There's a hint of smoke, high acidity and a medium, smooth finish. The latte is almost too hot; fortunately, the milk is well textured and retains some of its sweetness.

Phone
+613 9560 9705

Trading Hours
mon - fri: 7.30am - 11pm
sat - sun: 8am - 11pm

Cafe... 19/25
Coffee... 16/25
Dimattina Coffee

OUR KITCHEN TABLE
134 Burke Road, Malvern East

Rough, unpolished wood floors, colonial-style furniture and shabby-chic fixtures afford a country-home feel, and set Our Kitchen Table apart from the ultra-modern cafes that dominate this part of Melbourne. More distinctive yet, the tea-cup sculpture surrounding one of the light fittings is a particular talking point, and most of the customers seem to comment on it when they pay at the counter.

Staff are pleasant and helpful, happy to answer questions and go about their business without fanfare. (They're also happy to receive compliments about the sculpture.)

My espresso arrives in a deliberately (we assume) mismatched cup and saucer, relieved of the formality and over-branding of your slick urban joints. It has a light crema and an equally light aroma; bready tones emerge, with a thin mid/rear palate and a medium finish. Adding milk in the form of a latte lifts the coffee markedly; it's perfectly heated and a sweetness permeates. The bready tones are also accentuated, as is the finish. Definitely one for the milk-based drinkers.

Phone
+613 9886 0458

Trading Hours
tue - sun: 7.30am - 4.30pm
monday closed

Cafe... 18/25
Coffee... 17/25
Atomica

THE COFFEE HIT
Shop G217, Westfield Shoppingtown, Doncaster

Shopped-out fashionistas will find a caffeine hit here that's a cut above the usual shopping-centre offerings. This cafe takes coffee seriously: as well as grinding and roasting its own beans, The Coffee Hit sells beans, utensils and books.

Situated in a light-filled atrium near upmarket grocery stores, Coffee Hit has a classy fit-out of dark timber furniture, with space for prams and shopping bags. There's sandwiches and cakes for sale, but the coffee is the main attraction — and a genuine outer-suburban rival to inner-city institutions.

My very short espresso has an intense, spicy aroma that fills the mouth but fades quickly. In a long black, the initial tobacco aroma fades into a mellow, slightly earthy taste that doesn't linger, while the latte, full of caramel and nuts, is an easy-sipping palate pleaser. If only my credit card could recharge so easily.

Phone
+613 9840 7725

Trading Hours
sat - wed: 8.30am - 5pm
thur - fri: 8.30am - 8pm

Cafe... 17/25
Coffee... 16/25
The Coffee Hit Blend

MOCHA GREEN
361 Hawthorn Road, Caulfield

This small place is easy to miss from the car, but plenty of locals have found it out — even if Mocha Green is positioned on a slightly uninspiring Hawthorn Road strip. The décor is crisp and fresh, made mellow with dark-wood details, a glass-fronted display counter full of exquisite looking pastries, and a selection of Tea Drop teas for anyone not on the coffee bandwagon.

The Wega by the door hisses and steams as people grab takeaway orders through the window, nodding a hello to the flat out barista.

Despite the hustle, my Di Bella espresso still manages to catch me off guard. Thick and mellow in the mouth, it finishes with a surprising burst of biscuity caramel which makes the mouthful quite unexpected and delightful. And then a full cream latte proceeds to steal the show. With added milk, the burst of slightly bitter caramel becomes a longer toffee finish in the mouth. Milky and sweet, it's lovely and still, somehow, pleasantly unexpected.

Phone
+613 9532 9333

Trading Hours
mon - fri: 7am - 6.30pm
sat: 8am - 6.30pm
sunday closed

Cafe... 17/25
Coffee... 22/25
Di Bella Coffee

Outer Melbourne

CARRE STREET DELI
372 Glenhuntly Road, Elsternwick

Melbourne has a reputation as a food city, but good, small-scale delicatessens are a bit thin on the ground. Lucky, then, for this little gem. Don't be confused by the Glenhuntly Road address, Carre Street Deli is indeed, as the name suggests, on Carre Street, in the rear of a building that fronts the busier street. It's a bright and brisk little operation that provides something of a model for the reinvention of the old corner deli.

Happily, it also does a good coffee. Local roaster Espresso Syndicate provides the beans, and the short black is a spicy little number with an orange jam and chocolate complexion and a clove-laced aroma. A long, toffee-flavoured finish punctuates a bitter citrus brew with a truly superb creamy mouthfeel.

There's plenty of gourmet food including authentic Greek feta and Alligator brand pasta to cook at home, or you can sit in with a Portuguese custard tart and the papers on a stool at the large front windows. Let this be the future of delis everywhere.

Phone
+613 9532 8985

Trading Hours
mon - fri: 8.30am - 6pm
sat: 8.30am - 5pm
sun: 8.30am - 4pm

Cafe... 16/25
Coffee... 17/25
Espresso Syndicate

GRAVY TRAIN CAFE
83 Gamon Street, Yarraville

In a city that prides itself on tiny, tucked-away cafes and bars, Gravy Train Cafe is refreshingly spacious. Three separate areas offer plenty of room for groups, prams or pets: a shaded large front courtyard; the more cosy but buzzy inside room filled with posters about local activities; and a separate back area.

This cafe is not in busy Yarraville Village, but attracts its own share of locals and can be crowded at popular times. A lengthy menu offers breakfast until 4pm, along with lunch and a large selection of cakes.

Those who forego food and order "just a coffee" will still feel special, as it arrives on a tray with a glass of water. The bitter, earthy aroma of my short black fades away quickly, and the first sip reveals a treacly flavour and mouthfeel. The latte has no discernable aroma but it is quite sweet and enjoyable.

Phone
+613 9687 9866

Trading Hours
everyday: 7.30am - 5pm

Cafe... 16/25
Coffee... 16/25
Genovese Coffee

THE MALING ROOM
206 Canterbury Road, Canterbury

The Maling Room occupies the former post office building that stands sentinel at the end of Maling Road, Canterbury. It's a timber-surfaced, pram-and-gran-filled joint that brims with the chatter of locals, and attentive staff shimmy and smile through this eclectic mix.

As a micro-roaster, the Maling Room sells bags of single and mixed-estate beans from the likes of Kenya, Honduras, Indonesia and Colombia, and – if what they serve on site is anything to go by – it's worth picking up a bag as you leave.

My espresso is smooth, fruity and mellow, with rich viscosity and no trace of grit or acidity. The latte is sweet, creamy and mild, and is at the perfect temperature (the menu advises that milk is steamed at 60-65 °C. In fact, if you want a (too) hot latte you've got to ask for it specially.

The breakfast menu (served until 3pm) ranges from hangover cure – a bacon and HP sauce sarnie – to posh eggs drizzled with truffle oil. Make like a parcel and get there.

Phone
+613 9836 9889

Trading Hours
everyday: 7.30am - 5pm

Cafe... 23/25
Coffee... 23/25
The Maling Room

Outer Melbourne

BOSSY BOOTS
106 Bay Street, Brighton

Sitting confidently outside Bay Street's main drag, this homely but most definitely upmarket operation reflects all the goodness and heartiness of a country-style kitchen. Its neutral-beige interior is enlivened by the aroma of just-baked cakes and an enormous display window brimming with inventive, healthy comfort food: bright salads with plenty of veggies, arancini, fish cakes, savoury pastries and more.

We observe plenty of skinny lattes and plates piled high destined for Brighton ladies, whether kerbside, in the leafy courtyard, or at the communal table indoors. Warm front-of-house staff – a welcome mix of the young and the more mature – constantly interact with the four fully-uniformed chefs in the semi-open kitchen-cum-bakehouse.

My not-so-short black has an inviting floral fragrance, a mildness complemented by hints of cocoa, and a dark chocolate, bittersweet aftertaste. A friendly departure sees us laden with hearty provisions to help warm our own home kitchens.

Phone
+613 9596 6825

Trading Hours
mon - thur: 7am - 7pm
fri: 7am - 6pm
sat: 7.30am - 4pm
sunday closed

Cafe... 20/25
Coffee... 17/25
Coffee Supreme

BLOSSOM & VINE
13 South Road, Brighton

This tiny cafe, in its cluster of shops behind Brighton Beach train station, is as cute as its name. The understated décor, modest menu and somewhat slow service all suggest this is just your average bayside local. However, three things correct that impression.

First, although it's early on a Sunday morning, the place is full of locals tucking into insanely large servings of bacon and eggs. Second, from a very comfortable brown leather bench I take in stunning views of a sparking Port Phillip bay. Third, and most decisively, the coffee is exceptionally good.

A Gravity espresso wafts with an aroma of Middle Eastern spices, and on the first sip it smacks the palate with lively acidity. Rich flavours of roasted nuts and dark chocolate follow, although the aftertaste is overly bitter. My latte, however, is faultless. The sweet silkiness of the milk perfectly matches the coffee's punchy acidity. Softer hazelnut, almond and chocolate notes thrill my tastebuds and linger, leaving me contemplating another. This is not a book to judge by its cover.

Phone
+613 9592 2000

Trading Hours
mon - fri: 7.30am - 1pm
sat - sun: 8.30am - 3pm

Cafe... 18/25
Coffee... 18/25
Gravity Coffee

SNOW PONY CAFE
95 Whitehorse Road, Balwyn

It may be named after the address, or it might be a reference to the Alison Lester book of the same name perched on the counter — either way you'll be saying *Giddy-up!*

The décor exudes a studied air of the arty olde-world, from the communal table and industrial light-fittings to changing displays of artwork and jazz crooning in the background. Regulars are greeted by name, ordering buttery Noisette pastries or signature 'smashed avocado' breakfasts as we sneak through the Parisian-cafe middle room to the hidden back courtyard.

Here in the sunshine we sink into tart Allpress coffee. My neat espresso arrives short, dark and handsome, wafting roast walnuts. It wakes me up with a surprisingly bright, fresh tang followed by a sharp finish, and it's a decisive start to the day. The muted soy latte is mellower, with light nuttiness ending on a gently bitter note — a welcome accompaniment to sweet breakfast banana bread. Better order another round, because it looks like this pony's heading for a trifecta.

Phone
+613 9816 8911

Trading Hours
mon - fri: 8am - 4pm
sat - sun: 8.30am - 4pm

Cafe... 21/25
Coffee... 19/25
Allpress Espresso

Outer Melbourne

RED DOOR CORNER STORE
70 Mitchell Street, Northcote

As the name suggests, there's red door, and it was once a corner store. Today, it's like a Nanna's kitchen wonderland of baking bric-a-brac. Cooling racks, teapots and colanders vie for space like some olde-world show-and-tell, much of it in the signature red.

The front counter is piled high with glass bells of house-baked gingerbread, as well as sticky tarts and cakes. But behind these treats, the real star of the show rumbles away: a shiny La Marzocco. There's a queue of locals for the Gravity brew, and we're interested to note it's 20 cents off for BYO cups.

And on this corner, they make a mean, short macchiato. Arriving with a perfect white dot of milk froth, it fills the mouth with soft tones of scorched toffee, and lingers long on the palate. The nutty soy latte is no less of a joy, and teases with hints of roasted nuts. Better order some home-made crumpets and settle in for another round — and it's cash only, so come prepared.

Phone
+613 9489 8040

Trading Hours
mon - fri: 7am - 5pm
sat: 8am - 4pm
sun: 8am - 3pm

Cafe... 22/25
Coffee... 22/25
Gravity Coffee

THE BREAKFAST CLUB
206 St Georges Road, Northcote

Sitting at the communal table in The Breakfast Club, I let my hair fall into my face, Ally Sheedy style, and suddenly feel right at home. Fans of the eponymous film will know exactly what I mean — everyone else will just see a scruffy looking chick sipping a really excellent macchiato.

It may be named after that coming-of-age movie, but this tiny cafe has much more to recommend it. For a start it's got that 'share-house lounge room' charm of faded fabrics mixed with wicker chairs. It's also got a great menu (try the Brie and Quince Ringwald), as well as staff who are full of gentle smiles and relaxed attitude.

And finally, that Supreme short macchiato really is fantastic. Round and elegant, smooth with a hint of hazelnuts, it's the kind of coffee that's gone too quickly and demands another. So I settle in with a soy latte and find the nuttiness coming through again. It sure beats detention.

Trading Hours
mon - fri: 7.30am - 3pm
sat - sun: 9am - 3pm

Cafe... 18/25
Coffee... 20/25
Coffee Supreme

Have you tried a Grinders Coffee?

Grinders Coffee, Australia's fastest-growing coffee supplier was established in 1962 in Lygon Street, the centre of Melbourne's famous Italian quarter.

Committed to expanding through the use of leading-edge roasting and other coffee technology, our coffee is roasted daily in our state-of-the-art roasting plant in Fairfield, Victoria.

Our boutique range of coffees, from our original Brazil blend through to our European blend, can satisfy all palettes and tastes. We also offer a highly regarded Decaf blend and our Fair Trade Organic blend is Australian Certified Organic.

Grinders continues to strive to produce the highest-quality coffee blends for Australia's booming café and restaurant scene – and now for an increasingly astute domestic market.

Enjoy a Grinders Coffee today.

www.grinderscoffee.com.au   For all enquiries 1300 476 377

EDEN ESPRESSO
121 Glenferrie Road, Malvern

This place has funk by the bucket load, from brightly coloured chairs and mismatched benches to ultra-suave baristas and staff. Happily, it doesn't make the rest of us feel out of place, and it certainly doesn't overshadow the Golden Cobra fair trade, organic coffee.

Perch street-side and peruse the menu, or just watch the passing traffic of Glenferrie road — either way you're bound to see something you like. But if there's room in the quiet courtyard, settle on in. The barista is quick and efficient at his work, leaving just enough room for cheery banter if you're so inclined.

He delivers a piping hot espresso, full of earthy and resinous aromas. It's dark and oily in the cup, with a rusty, stiff crema that provides a sharp tang before giving in to a mellowness. A super smooth latte romances me more gently with a perfect milk-to-coffee balance. Eden by name… and yes, garden of earthy delights by nature.

Phone
+613 9509 9119

Trading Hours
mon - thur: 7am - 6pm
fri: 7am - 10pm
sat - sun: 8am - 10pm

Cafe... 19/25
Coffee... 19/25
Golden Cobra

MAIN STREET
505 Main Street, Mordialloc

The birth of Main Street in late '09 saw cafe culture come alive on this otherwise ho-hum 'Mordy' streetscape. Pulsating in the town's heart near the train station, this magnetic meeting place dispenses warmth, conviviality and the occasional hug with every shot from its blood-red, four-group Ruggero.

More than a cafe, this licensed one-stop-shop does everything from beer on tap and coffee to big brekkies, lunches and dinners — all great Mod Oz tucker. It's airy and stylish, yet makes casual space with alfresco sipping, supping and socialising options. Cellar-like textures and hues (exposed, original brickwork, warm timbers and wine-barrel light fittings) are dramatically punctuated by startling splashes of red coffee cups.

My espresso presents a rich, caramel-sweet aroma. Its initial edginess is chased by a full, round flavour with a hint of hazelnuts and a mellow finish. Savouring its long, sweet aftertaste, my veins pulse with renewed life-blood — much like Main Street itself. And it's about time.

Phone
+613 9580 8150

Trading Hours
mon - fri: 6.30am - late
sat - sun: 7.30am - late

Cafe... 20/25
Coffee... 17/25
Dimattina Coffee

ARTFUL DODGER
267 Glenhuntly Road, Elsternwick

"Please, Sir, I want some more." This licensed newcomer charms you into return visits, through both its selection of four deftly-executed Di Bella grinds (Ali, Modena, Organic and Decaffeinated), and its "food glorious food".

Like the character, it's infectious, with a large alfresco area overlooking the street, and a *Happy Days* soda shoppe-like exterior. Stepping into the small cafe with starburst lighting and zigzag-panelled ceiling, we're warmly welcomed — and not only by the four gleaming grinders. Standouts on the innovative breakfast and lunch menu include Dodger's Gruel of Quinoa Porridge, Coconut Milk and Mango, a selection of Convent Bakery baguettes, and Caramelised Shallot and Taleggio Tart. Not to mention the cocktails.

An award-winning espresso is bright and full-bodied, its initially sweet berry resolving into velvety toffee. We finish with a Modena latte, its fragrance, vibrancy and caramel chocolate tones silencing all begging.

Phone
+613 9523 5541

Trading Hours
mon - wed: 6.30am - 5pm
thur - sun: 6.30am - 10pm

Cafe... 21/25
Coffee... 19/25
Di Bella Coffee

Outer Melbourne

THE PICKLE BARREL DELI
60 Ferguson Street, Williamstown

Despite the name, there's nothing vinegary about this tiny deli-cafe. Instead, subtle lighting, exposed brick walls and dark furniture create a cosy atmosphere, while bold red accents provide a touch of spice. Add the stream of regulars chatting to the friendly barista over the shiny Wega machine, and you know you're onto a good thing.

Like any good condiment, The Pickle Barrel Deli also packs a punch in the flavour stakes. The menu comprises largely rustic fare (think Wild Mushroom Quiche or Chunky Raspberry and Rhubarb Tart), while the small deli at the rear offers gourmet essentials such as olives, charcuterie and other delights — pomegranate molasses, anyone?

But it's the coffee that really shines. Hiding below a thick caramel crema, my espresso is beautifully balanced. Rich and syrupy on the tongue, its subtle toffee undertones give way to a short velvety finish. A dash of milk rounds out the acidity, letting the natural sweetness tantalise the palate. We'll be back.

Phone
+613 9399 8338

Trading Hours
mon - fri: 7am - 6pm
sat - sun: 7am - 4pm

Cafe... 19/25
Coffee... 20/25
Genovese Coffee

APTE (A Place To Eat)
538 Heidelberg Road, Alphington

The creative conversion of old milk bars is one of the happy side-effects of the otherwise lamentable demise of the neighbourhood corner store. Apte is a prime example — and a very popular one at that. Located on Heidelberg Road, this bright and breezy cafe has an enthusiastic young staff, a crisp, clean fit-out and a gorgeous sunny courtyard garden.

My espresso is big on the palate, all citrusy orange and clove, with an inky viscosity, reasonably short finish and mid-bitter aftertaste. The latte is less impressive, mainly due to a coarse crema and slightly overcooked milk.

There is a suitably reliable, if not terribly adventurous dining menu that certainly proves a winner with the locals. The biggest complaint, however, is the road noise. An investment in a sound-dampening front fence would pay lovely, tranquil dividends.

Phone
+613 9482 2991

Trading Hours
everyday: 8am - 4pm

Cafe... 17/25
Coffee... 14/25
5 Senses Coffee

NOSH @ NEWPORT
24 Hall Street, Newport

Just like a university share-house, Nosh@Newport is an unspoken central meeting point for people looking to relax and chat with mates — or recover from a hard night's partying. Unashamedly cheap and cheerful décor only adds to this atmosphere, making it feel more like a large living room than a cafe.

The all-day breakfast menu has a variety of hearty options, defiantly catering more to those suffering from a hangover than to health nuts. The staff are friendly and attentive, even though the cafe is close to full.

I can smell the espresso before it arrives at the table. Its strong aroma has a huge hit of chocolate, as well as some milder spice and earthy notes. The crema is an incredibly rich and inviting dark speckled brown. The taste is nothing short of spectacular: beautifully rounded and balanced, but still light and bright enough to quaff in one hit. A citrus tang adds to the finish perfectly.

Phone
+613 9391 6404

Trading Hours
mon - thur: 7am - 4pm
fri: 7am - 11pm
sat: 8am - 11pm
sun: 8am - 4pm

Cafe... 20/25
Coffee... 21/25
Coffee Supreme

Outer Melbourne

LB.2
Shop 2/1 Carre Street, Elsternwick

Coffee, like any comestible, is such a fickle thing to review. One man's Grange can be another man's raspberry cordial. Just so, the coffee at Lb.2 won't be to everyone's taste. It is big, bold, boisterous and bitter.

The roast is by Gravity; the preparation and presentation are good; and it's well extracted and caramel/ochre in colour. Its aroma suggests this espresso is no shrinking violet, and the release on the palate is joyous and forthright. A great way to start the day. Naturally, it mellows in a milky concoction, but even the latte is uncompromising.

The cafe itself is a contemporary space with lots of hard surfaces and straight lines, and the staff is very cheery, knowledgeable and enthusiastic. There is outdoor seating, a winning menu and a cruisy vibe. It's a shame the cafe is in the shade for most of the day, but late in the afternoon the western sun can light the terrace.

Phone
+613 9528 6440

Trading Hours
mon - sat: 7.30am - 4pm
sun: 8am - 4pm

Cafe... 18/25
Coffee... 16/25
Gravity Coffee

SALOOP
151 Martin Street, Brighton

Its name might have come from the dark ages, but this Brighton favourite speaks of modern cool. White tables and funky lime-green chairs brighten up the ho-hum of the Martin Street drag and mark the entrance to this fun, child-friendly cafe. While ordering, I'm distracted by an alluring assortment of fresh muffins, friands, and lemon meringue pies, but it's a pure caffeine fix I'm here for.

As it's a fine sunny Sunday, the two sun-drenched rooms are almost full of happily brunching families and bayside hip young things. I'm content with a table at the back where I can soak up the relaxed vibe.

The coffee matches the mood. My espresso is topped by golden sand crema and breezes with flowers and grass. An initial roundness gives way to a splash of wild orange. With milk though, the delicate flavour of the coffee is slightly drowned out, but nonetheless leaves an easygoing sweetness on the palate.

Phone
+613 9596 6944

Trading Hours
mon - fri: 7am - 4.30pm
sat - sun: 8am - 4pm

Cafe... 19/25
Coffee... 15/25
Gigante

BAMBALEROS
84 Maling Road, Canterbury

Tucked into the pretty precinct of Canterbury's Maling Road shops, Bambaleros is a happy breather from knick-knacks and lace. The proud roaster on display touts the virtue of fair-trade coffee, and offers some excellent tasting notes to boot.

A long macchiato arrives with an unexpectedly voluminous white froth — more cappuccino than 'stain' of milk — with a slightly charry finish stealing through the otherwise biscuit tones. But happily, the latte is more impressive, with heavy creaminess marrying well to the baked notes and finishing with a malty flourish.

There's a lot of information here, and a nod to various coffee drinking cultures, along with images of coffee cherries and clear dispensers filled with beans (Ethiopian Limu and Colombian Swiss Water Decaf). You can also choose from a wide array of cleaners, plungers and grinders to help at home. And, thankfully, there's also plenty of advice on hand — all you have to do is ask.

Phone
+613 9836 5385

Trading Hours
mon: 9.30am - 4pm
tue - sun: 9.30am - 4.30pm

Cafe... 19/25
Coffee... 16/25
Bambaleros

NORTHCOTE COFFEE BAR
Shop 6/224 St Georges Road, Northcote

Northcote Coffee Bar is not here to excite you. Nor to romanticise your Saturday morning. And it's certainly not here to provide a cosy place to linger over a lazy latte or three. It's here to serve a need. The cafe consists of a main-road shop offering a small range of standard meals (ham, cheese and tomato croissants, or a selection of freshly made panini) and good coffee. Nothing more, nothing less.

Attention to interior design is negligible: polished concrete floor, bland furniture, off-white mosaic splashback, and a combination of sliding glass doors and a low ceiling that seems to amplify every car speeding by. But if you're in one of said cars and hankering for a quick bite or quality caffeine hit, then screech to a halt right here.

The coffee has a pleasing weight to it; the dense, golden crema and full-bodied espresso combine to deliver a well-balanced short black with citrus notes and a fresh, almost herbaceous aftertaste.

Phone
+613 9489 8045

Trading Hours
everyday: 7am - 4pm

Cafe... 11/25
Coffee... 17/25
Bean Ground & Drunk

Outer Melbourne

PEABERRYS
269 Charman Road, Cheltenham

Eyes widen at the splendid sight of a roaster turning and whirring, while the mind goes every which way with the choice of blends, some single-origin and many fair trade. And in suburban Cheltenham — who would've thought!

A good breakfast and lunch menu pairs up with Sweet by Nature cakes. Coffee, however, is the indisputable star in this ethical home of Gigante Coffee, which was first established in Highett in 1993 as 'San Remo Coffee' and one of Melbourne's first roasteries.

Given its justifiably back- rather than front-of-house focus, we order the gold medal-winning Fairtrade blend at the counter. Barista Charles Skadiang extracts and delivers it with attentiveness and finesse. And I'm lifted to new heights by its fragrant, nutty aroma, the earthy, mildly-spiced sweetness, and deliciously long-lingering creamy milk chocolate aftertaste. Sheer brilliance.

Phone
+613 9583 2766

Trading Hours
mon - fri: 7am - 5pm
sat - sun: 8am - 1pm

Cafe... 14/25
Coffee... 22/25
Gigante

LOCO COFFEE
436 Glenhuntly Road, Elsternwick

Welcome to the old curiosity shop! Ladders support strings of teapots, signposts flash proclamations across the walls, and big chunky benches abound. Part coffee museum, part bric-a-brac store, everything at Loco Coffee is a little battered but bursting with enthusiasm.

Waiters bustle to and fro, regulars crack loud jokes, and a glass-fronted museum piece of a display case holds a drool-inducing ensemble of caramel biscuits. It's hard not to feel totally at home here, especially if you order the eggs on hash — a real hangover special.

The coffee is just another reason to settle in. My espresso is smooth and well balanced, mellow with a hint of woodiness which suits the surrounds. And the latte is an artwork in itself: from the thick, full body to the soft milk-chocolate finish, not to mention the delicate face etched into the milk froth. The barista clearly loves his art, and so do we.

Phone
+613 9532 4455

Trading Hours
everyday: 7am - 5.30pm

Cafe... 19/25
Coffee... 17/25
Di Bella Coffee

YOUR BARISTA NEEDS YOU

Each day an army of baristas supply us with our caffeine needs. It's time we give something back.

Nominate your favourite barista by logging on to our website. The barista with the most nominations will be featured in the next edition of The Coffee Guide...

www.thecoffeeguide.com.au

Melbourne 2011 Award Winners

Five Bean Winners

65 Degrees
Page 9

St Ali Coffee Roasters
Page 47

Monk Bodhi Dharma
Page 77

Dukes Coffee Roasters
Page 33

Proud Mary
Page 67

Market Lane Coffee
Page 83

Seven Seeds
Page 43

Three Bags Full
Page 75

The Maling Room
Page 141

God Shot

(divine intervention – in espresso form)

WINNER
65 Degrees
Page 9

RUNNER-UP
Proud Mary
Page 67

Best Newcomer
(the brew kids on the block)

WINNER
Market Lane Coffee
Page 83

RUNNER-UP
Monk Bohdi Dharma
Page 77

Best Cafe Design
(it's more than tables and chairs)

WINNER
Seven Seeds
Page 43

RUNNER-UP
Dukes Coffee Roasters
Page 33

Best Breakfast
(food that gets you out of bed)

WINNER
Three Bags Full
Page 75

RUNNER-UP
Proud Mary
Page 67

Beyond the Call of Duty
(to those who take coffee beyond lip service)

WINNER
Proud Mary
Page 67

RUNNER-UP
Market Lane Coffee
Page 83

Sydney 2011 Edition

Five Bean Cafes

Campos Coffee

Grind

Le Monde

Little Marionette

Mecca Espresso

Single Origin Roasters

The Bunker

For individual category winners, and the chance to nominate your favourite cafe visit

www.thecoffeeguide.com.au

Todays specials

www.thecoffeeguide.com.au has become interactive. Log on to discover new features. Join the guide to *find*... the perfect *grind*.

Guide Menu

Rate my cafe

Who do you think deserves 5 Beans? Rate your favourite venue just like *The Coffee Guide Team*.

Cafe of the week

Each week we'll feature a cafe from each publication. Log on and share your experience of that venue.

Daily Buzz...

The Coffee Guide... forum is open to all. Join in the discussion and tell us what you really think.

www.thecoffeeguide.com.au

DIRECTORY

ABBOTSFORD
Convent Bakery — pg 46
First Pour — pg 50
Three Bags Full — pg 75

ALBERT PARK
Dundas Place Cafe — pg 62

ALPHINGTON
APTE — pg 148

ARMADALE
Woodstock — pg 118

ASCOT VALE
Little Byrd — pg 80

BALACLAVA
Batch Espresso — pg 35
Coffee Company — pg 74
Midali — pg 46
Monk Bodhi Dharma — pg 77
Wall Two80 — pg 40

BALWYN
Snow Pony — pg 143

BALWYN NORTH
Caffe Romeo — pg 132

BRIGHTON
Blossom & Vine — pg 142
Bossy Boots — pg 142

BRIGHTON
Pod Espresso — pg 126
Rupert & the Fig — pg 135
Saloop — pg 150

BRUNSWICK
Brunswick Flour Mill — pg 81
Cafe 3A — pg 40
Minimo — pg 87
Ray Cafe — pg 88
Toby's Estate — pg 84

BRUNSWICK EAST
A Minor Place — pg 48
Brunswick East Project — pg 89
Small Block — pg 44

CAMBERWELL
Butterfly Cafe — pg 86
Collective Espresso — pg 85

CANTERBURY
Bombaleros — pg 151
Cornelius — pg 125
The Maling Room — pg 141

CARLTON
Brunetti — pg 74
Carlton Espresso — pg 34
Seven Seeds — pg 43

CARLTON NORTH
North — pg 84

CAULFIELD
Mocha Green — pg 139

CHELTENHAM
Peaberrys — pg 152

CLIFTON HILL
Mixed Business — pg 35

COLLINGWOOD
Proud Mary — pg 67

DONCASTER
Coffee Hit — pg 139

ELSTERNWICK
Artful Dodger — pg 147
Carre Street Deli — pg 140
Izzi Espresso — pg 134
Lb.2 — pg 150
Loco Coffee — pg 152

ESSENDON
MJ Forty Cafe — pg 122

FITZROY
Arcadia — pg 50
Atomica — pg 66
Babka Bakery Cafe — pg 68
Beans & Bagels — pg 82
Min Lokal — pg 72
Newtown SC — pg 42

"DO IT FOR YOURSELF

DIRECTORY

FITZROY NORTH
Growers Espresso pg 65
Julio pg 88

FLEMINGTON
Made pg 82
Social Roasting Co. pg 49

GLENHUNTLY
Cafe Whyte pg 132

GLEN WAVERLY
Coco Lounge pg 138

HAMPTON
Espresso Elements pg 137

HAWTHORN
Liar Liar pg 73
Porgie + Mr Jones pg 86
Sasa's Cafe pg 42

HEIDELBERG
Vyve Cafe pg 122

KENSINGTON
Elevenses pg 80
Luncheonette pg 62

KEW
Studio Movida pg 120
Wild Toast pg 124

MALVERN
Eden Espresso pg 146
Thread Cafe pg 136

MALVERN EAST
Our Kitchen Table pg 138

MELBOURNE CBD
65 Degrees pg 9
Bambini Barista pg 11
BBB pg 24
Brood Box pg 26
Cafenatics pg 22
Coffea Coffee pg 16
Coffee HQ pg 12
Coffee HQ (Flinders) pg 21
Cumulus Inc. pg 19
Cup of Truth (C.O.T) pg 27
Dancing Goat pg 8
D'Marco's pg 16
Eclipse pg 18
Espressino pg 15
Home Barista Institute pg 23
Jungle Juice Bar pg 20
Liaison pg 26
Ludo Cafe pg 12
Mess Hall pg 14
Negroni pg 20
Pellegrini's pg 10
Pushka Espresso Bar pg 21
Quist's Coffee pg 8
Red Cup Cafe pg 10
Roast and Brew pg 18
Sensory Lab pg 13

MELBOURNE CBD
Social Roasting Co. pg 22
Stax pg 14
Switchboard pg 24
Two Fingers pg 11

MENTONE
Truly Scrumptious pg 124

MIDDLE PARK
Mart 130 pg 48

MOONEE PONDS
Little Kitch pg 78
Nabiha pg 69
The Rusty Duck pg 36
Young Street Cafe pg 36

MORDIALLOC
Main Street pg 146

NEWPORT
Nosh @ Newport pg 149
Odd Spot pg 118

NORTH MEBOURNE
Appetite Cafe pg 58
Auction Rooms pg 63
Di Bella Roasting
Warehouse pg 51

"DO IT FOR YOUR COFFEE"

DIRECTORY

NORTHCOTE
Foxy Brown — pg 121
Northcote Coffee Bar — pg 151
Palomino — pg 120
Penny Farthing — pg 119
Red Door Corner Store — pg 144
The Breakfast Club — pg 144

PARKVILLE
Primary — pg 34

PORT MELBOURNE
Seven A.M. — pg 90

PRAHRAN
Piccolo Espresso — pg 57
Spoonful — pg 68

RICHMOND
7 Grams — pg 72
Chimmy's — pg 64
Espresso 3121 — pg 57
New York Tomato — pg 78

SEDDON
Cafe Le Chien — pg 119
Seddon Deadly Sins — pg 125

SOUTH MELBOURNE
Brazil Lifestyle Coffee — pg 66
Dead Man Espresso — pg 59
Dimattina Cafe — pg 76
Fratelli — pg 58

SOUTH MELBOURNE
Not All There — pg 52
Padre — pg 44
St Ali Coffee Roasters — pg 47

SOUTH YARRA
Lawson Grove Shop — pg 41
Market Lane Coffee — pg 83
Outpost By St Ali — pg 76

SPOTSWOOD
Duchess of Spotswood — pg 127

ST KILDA
Leroy Espresso — pg 64
Nineteen Squares — pg 52

THORNBURY
Crunch Cafe — pg 136

WEST MELBOURNE
Home Barista Institute — pg 90

WILLIAMSTOWN
Pickle Barrel — pg 148

WINDSOR
Dukes Coffee Roasters — pg 33

YARRAVILLE
Cornershop — pg 123
Feedback Cafe — pg 126
Gravy Train — pg 140
Hausfrau — pg 134

www.clubequal.com

Information

Ticketing zones
- Zone 1
- Zone 2
- Nearest tram station
- Connecting bus
- Tram terminus

For train, tram and bus information call
131 638/ **(TTY) 9619 2727** (6am–midnight daily)
or visit **metlinkmelbourne.com.au**

For Yarra Trams customer feedback and lost
property call **1800 800 166** (6am–midnight daily)
or visit **yarratrams.com.au**

Routes: 1, 3 (Mon–Fri),
3a (Sat–Sun), 5, 6, 8, 11,
16, 19, 24 (AM/PM peaks),
30, 42, 48, 55, 57, 59, 64, 67, 70,
72, 75, 78 (until 7pm), 79 (after 7pm),
82, 86, 95 (Mon–Fri), 96, 109, 112

© State of Victoria, 2010

NORTH

MAP NOT TO SCALE
Effective 25 July 2010

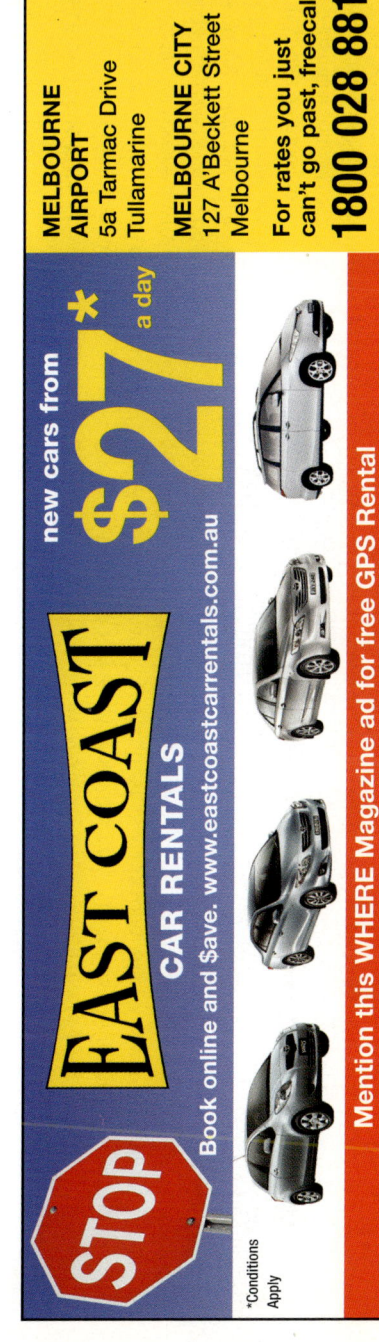

MELBOURNE IS FULL of fantastic attractions that offer something for everyone no matter what your age or interests. For wildlife lovers there are such delights as Melbourne Zoo, Healesville Sanctuary, Werribee Open Range Zoo, Melbourne Aquarium and Phillip Island.

If you're a garden lover then a visit to the Australian Garden and Royal Botanic Gardens are a must. Into history? Well then you should include the Melbourne Museum, Scienceworks, the Immigration Museum, Cooks' Cottage, the Shrine of Remembrance and Melbourne's many National Trust properties on your itinerary. Love art – well then make sure you include a stop at the National Gallery of Victoria. For sports lovers there are such wonderful attractions as Etihad Stadium, the Melbourne Cricket Ground and Rod Laver Arena.

One of the best ways to get a feel of Melbourne is from Eureka Skydeck 88, which offers great views over the city. Then jump onto the City Circle tram. Not only will you see the city from 'ground level' but also enjoy one of Melbourne's iconic experiences – a tram ride.

If you've only got limited time in the city, or you need some help with planning and booking, make sure you speak to your concierge, who is not only extremely knowledgeable and helpful, but who can organise your excursions for you.

Melbourne cityscape by John Gollings. Image courtesy Federation Square.

WHERE TO GO
in Melbourne

MELBOURNE TRAM NETWORK

Melbourne tram network

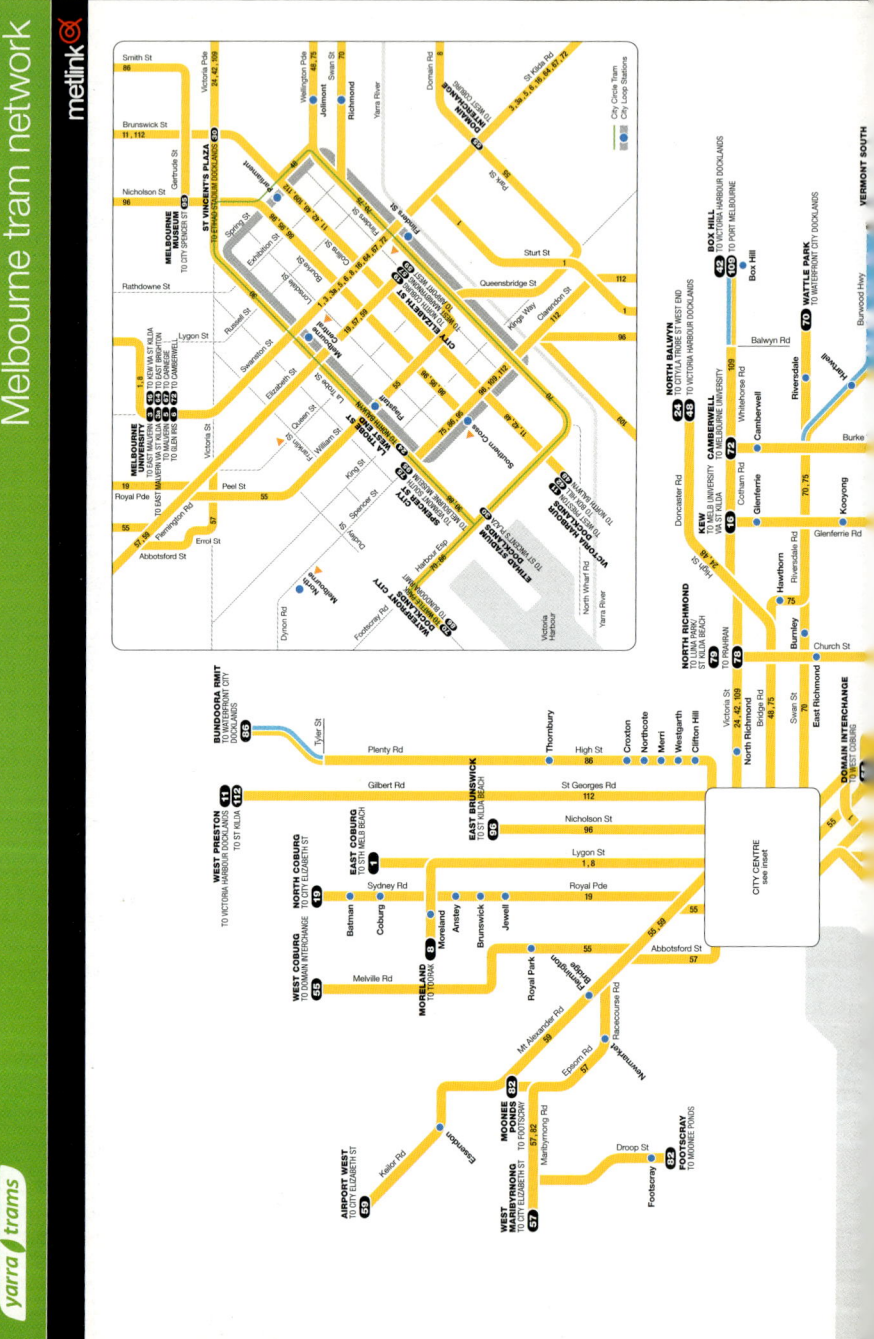